Floating Low to Lofoten

Martin Edge

This nonsense is dedicated to my Dad, Myles Edge. When he started sailing it was a properly difficult and uncomfortable activity. He'd have loved to have made a trip like this and would have made a better fist of it than me.

Floating Low to Lofoten

Zophiel's Cruise in 2008

Martin Edge

First Print Edition 2014
Published in Great Britain 2011 by Martin Edge.
Copyright © Martin Edge 2011

The full sets of colour pictures from this and other volumes of Zophiel's travels are available free at:

http://www.edge.me.uk

Table of Contents

Preface

This is the holiday journal of a floating, ranting wimp. It is the tale of that wimp's progress round the seas of northern Europe.

In 2003 I bought a small and slightly scruffy yacht called 'Zophiel'. Though rather small for long distance cruising, the cutter rigged Vancouver is a seaworthy heavyweight. The first one was designed for a couple of nutters who were emigrating from Canada to New Zealand and wanted to do it in a 27ft sailing boat. Other Vancouvers have crossed oceans and sailed round the world.

My ambitions are rather more modest. Actually that's not true. I'd love to join the ranks of the fearless ocean navigators and sail round the world. But, as I've already mentioned, I'm a bit of a wimp. So over the past few years I've spent summers cruising around parts of northern Europe from Zophiel's base near Edinburgh. Most of these journeys have been sailed solo but I've had a crew for the longer sea crossings. Again, I'm no Robin Knox-Johnston. 'Floating Low to Lofoten' is the tale of the second of these trips, in the summer of 2008.

I started out writing a straightforward description of the trip, but the account grew arms and legs and kept on expanding. The problem was that the coast of Norway is entirely gorgeous and the further north you go the more fabulous and surprising it gets. I couldn't stop myself from waxing lyrical. It's not just the landscape that's surprising. In Scotland we are told that we're too small a country, too far north and with a landscape too barren to be productive. We are conditioned to think of our northern and western fringes as wastelands where there's no prospect of a proper economy or thriving communities. The drain of migration from the north and the west is supposed to be as natural as a river flowing out to the sea. Then I went to Norway, with a smaller population and a much, much longer and more remote coastline than Scotland. Right up to seventy degrees north, way above the Arctic Circle, there's a thriving town round every headland. There's people and industry. There's numerous ships plying the sheltered waters transporting goods and people and fish and bits of North Sea oil platform. Ten degrees north of the last viable tree in Scotland there's deciduous forests sheltering the suburban streets of proper little towns.

So I hope this account of a sailing trip, as well as being reasonably entertaining, will give some pause for thought about a few issues, even though it's just the ramblings of a holidaying wimp.

Floating Low to Lofoten is the follow-up to "Skagerrak and Back", which described Zophiel's 2007 North Sea circuit. "A Gigantic Whinge on the Celtic Fringe" is an account of her 2011 circumnavigation of Ireland and "Bobbing to the Baltic" is the tale of her trip to the Russian Border with Finland in 2012.

Martin Edge, December 2011

A Day-Sail on the Forth

Having done a sort of circuit of the North Sea the previous year – starting by crossing to Bergen and going south and clockwise, I'd determined that the west coast of Norway was to be my cruising ground this year. I thought I'd head north this time. Early on I was discussing my plans for the trip with a friend at Port Edgar marina on the Forth when he asked me how far north I'd go in Norway. Desperately dredging my brain for its limited knowledge of Norwegian geography I said *'Oh, I don't know, probably up to the Lofoten Islands'*. He seemed surprised and impressed. It wasn't until I'd bought the hundred or so charts necessary to get to Lofoten that I realised just how bleedin' far it is up the coast of Norway.

A 27 footer, however well designed for ocean crossing, is a relatively small boat to do the trip on and the previous year Zophiel had seemed pretty small amongst the forty-plus footers of monied Scandinavia. Vancouvers are also not Norway's commonest yacht. This year she was to seem even smaller and yet more obscure. In my three months spent cruising the length of Norway in 2008 only one person recognised the Vancouver for what she was, though it was a person of some discernment. But more of that later.

In early May 2008 we'd had the usual easterlies and a haar - the seasonal sea fog that plagues the east coast for some time. I was waiting for a weather window to begin the trip. On May 6th we still had easterlies but there was no fog forecast, so I thought I'd make a start moving Zophiel north in stages. I told

Anna, my other half, that I'd probably be back home that evening – or at the latest the following night – and headed down to Port Edgar for a wee sail. I beat out through the Forth Road and Rail bridges with the last of the falling tide against a rising easterly and wondered if

The Forth Rail Bridge

Escort into Stonehaven

I might just sail four miles round the nearby island of Inchcolm and back.

I didn't really mean to end up in Shetland. I had intended to start shifting Zophiel northwards in preparation for a crossing to Norway in June. I thought perhaps at the most I might do a couple of day sails the thirty miles to Anstruther and another twenty five or so to Arbroath, where I could leave her for a week or so until the next wee push north. However with a rising easterly to batter into that morning it was most likely to be a wee day sail and back to Port Edgar. It certainly didn't feel like the auspicious start of a 2800 mile cruise. As I was casting off I told the guy on the boat next to Zoph in the marina that I'd probably be back that evening after a wee sail, and headed off.

But in the second week of May 2008 every day dawned bright and sunny with anything from a moderate south-easterly to nothing at all, so every day I kept going and ended up unexpectedly at over 60 degrees north in Lerwick.

Perhaps that's the best way to start a cruise – casually and without even letting on to yourself that the odyssey has started. Just let it creep up on you and suddenly find that you are hundreds of miles from home. That way you can fool the weather gods who would otherwise fling two weeks of contrary gales your way if you were properly organised and had announced that you were heading out on a particular date.

The other way to guarantee good weather, of course, is to be in league with the devil like Gordon Campion. Two years previously Gordon had sailed his Moody 38 'Equinox' from the Forth round Spitzbergen and Back, reaching over 80 degrees north. I'd crewed for him for the leg from Tromsø to Bergen. This trip, a lot of which was offshore and didn't involve a lot of stopping, had given me a taste for northern Norway.

Unlike most of us, Gordon seems able to run a sailing cruise like a Swiss train timetable. He plans ahead for up to two years and leaves and arrives exactly when he says he will. Crucially the weather - and this is the bit where he's in league with the devil - always behaves for him.

When I joined him in Tromsø he was proudly waving a ten day forecast he'd just got from the Norwegian Met Office up the hill in town. Some eight days later, at sea, I suggested that it was about time we had a look at a weather forecast. Puzzled, Gordon waved the ten day forecast, now more than a week out of date. "But we've got the forecast" he said. "On Tuesday afternoon it'll be blowing force 3 from the north east".

I protested that this isn't how the world works. You can't rely on an eight day old forecast. But Gordon can. He proved the point by sailing Equinox round the world between 2008 and 2010. Again he set the schedule long in advance and stuck to it rigidly. The weather consistently dealt him its proper seasonal average conditions everywhere he went.

For ordinary mortals it's better not to be too categorical about our plans. One of the best reasons for imaging the existence of a god is so that you can make the joke: "What's the best way of making God laugh? Tell him your plans".

That first morning the tide and a beat under full sail took me out past Burntisland. As the tide turned, the wind increased to a high force 4 or low 5 on the nose and time started pressing. So this turned into a wet blatter of a motorsail into the five foot swell. But on a sunny day a few wee splashes of salt water aren't the problem they can be on a grey, overcast one.

I was heading for the attractive Fife town of Pittenweem on the recommendation of John Murphy, the skipper of Port Edgar's biggest boat, a Jeanneau 49 called Erin. He had assured people on numerous occasions that, contrary to the warnings in the pilot book, they'd receive a warm welcome there.

"This is a commercial harbour, yachts are not allowed in. Anyway, you wouldn't stay afloat. Go to Anstruther" said the Harbour Master when I phoned him a couple of hours before arriving. Even when I lied a little and said I mightn't make it to Anstruther before the tide fell I was told it wasn't his problem and, politely enough, to bugger off. Perhaps it's Erin's well stocked cellar that appeases the Harbour Master, but I think John tends to look at all the wee harbours on the Forth with somewhat rose-tinted cheeks.

The last time I was in Anstruther, a few years ago, it was to lean against the harbour wall. Not any more. The drying harbour is now full of pontoons which make it difficult for fin keelers, particularly at springs. The pontoons are however raised above the thin mud by steel frames, so for a long keeler like Zoph, with a moderate draught, it's easy enough to lean gently against this platform when it dries out, if you tie the lines right and have plenty of fenders. I had been told – again by Cap'n Erin – who's champagne flute is always at least half full - that we would sink comfortably into deep mud here. That's not the case. The bottom is quite hard – hardcore having been laid down when the pontoons were installed according to one local – but the pontoons are designed to be leaned against. Kipping at a 15° heel notwithstanding, a comfortable enough night was had at Ainster.

Part of the reason to plough into the wind to Anstruther had been the forecasted shift to gentle south-easterlies, which would be ideal once round Fife Ness and heading north. So the next morning it was a motorsail on a falling tide north towards Stonehaven. The sun would again have been knocking down the dykes were there such thing as dykes in the sea off the Tay Estuary.

Within five miles of Stonehaven the traditional east coast three bottlenose dolphin escort joined me for half an hour's frolic around Zoph's bow. They criss-crossed from side to side, throwing in the occasional leap just to show off, as I sat in the bow 3 feet above them getting burned by the sun. Just occasionally

you can sail up the East
coast of Scotland thinking
'Pah! The Caribbean, who
needs it?' and mean it.

Stonehaven Harbour

In Stonehaven I tied
up in the outer harbour
near an eight metre
speedboat which had
conspired to take up most
of the mooring space
usually available to about
four boats and which,
apparently, had broken down. Later I was joined by a fine 45ft steel Dutch yacht.

The next day I headed north for Peterhead in another scorcher, sailing part
of the way but motor-sailing once Zoph dropped below three knots. Having
lived in Aberdeen for 16 years it's always a surprise to sail in full sun past some
of its shittiest bits and realise that none of the poor sods that live there ever
experience how nice it can be only a mile or so away out at sea.

As I approached Peterhead harbour a wee motor boat zipped past me –
unnecessarily close I thought – and I recognised it as the one which had been
broken down in Stonehaven. He contacted port control on the VHF to request
entry - making a bit of an arse of it – and I followed suit.

Any brief feeling of jealousy I might have had at the speed with which he
could get there from Stonehaven was quickly dispelled by the ensuing dramatic
and daring sea rescue. He came on the radio again to say that his engine had
broken down and that he was anchored in the middle of the harbour. Harbour
Control suggested that the yacht which was following him in – that is Zoph -
might like to assist and I called up to say I'd give him a tow. I only just got there
before a couple of wee fishing boats who's crews, I suspect, scented salvage and
weren't there out of the kindness of their hearts. I chucked him a tow line and
waited while he disentangled his anchor from a load of lobster pots, then towed
him into the marina.

I thought I recognised the skipper and it transpired he was the same bloke
I'd helped with his lines a couple of times in Port Edgar. He suffered repeatedly
from two problems – a lot of windage on his top heavy, shallow draft boat and
the complete inability to work out which rope to tie where to stop her blowing
away. Tied up in Peterhead marina I pointed out to him that his bow was
actually repeatedly banging up against one of the electricity and water towers
on the pontoon. Though unconcerned he did say that he'd sort this problem out.
A while later I was incredulous as I noticed that he'd simply taken the step of
tying a fender to the bow, so that now the fender smashed repeatedly against
the leccy tower. It never seemed to enter his mind that perhaps the lines needed

adjusting. A relaxed approach to tying a boat to a pontoon reminiscent of Norway. I began to feel I was almost there already.

It did strike me that heading up the east coast with a single engine and no backup motive force was asking for trouble and that he had been extraordinarily lucky to break down in Peterhead harbour, as opposed to a mile out to sea off some rocks. When he went off to the pub I went over and retied his boat for him, mostly to prevent him knocking over the leccy meter and causing a blackout.

The rest of the day was spent trying to find a shop that sold food in the desolate, ostensibly post-apocalyptic streets of Peterhead. It is a universal truth that you can't buy food in the centre of cities, only shoes and clothes. The entire economy of a planet written about by Douglas Adams collapsed because the urban areas relied entirely on shoe sales and the situation on planet Earth isn't much better. If you want food, tie up in a wee village, not a town. If you want to buy anything at all, don't go to Peterhead. In the evening I entertained a work colleague to a couple of beers on board. I happened to meet him in the street. For some reason he, apparently voluntarily, lives in Peterhead.

Kirkwall Sunset

Brompting on Stronsay

The forecast looked fine for rounding Rattray head the next day, with gently south-easterlies increasing during the day. Of course the tidal window meant leaving at bleeding four a.m., but doesn't it always? Having motorsailed round Rattray Head by seven a.m. it struck me that I'd be in my chosen destination, Whitehills, by about eleven in the morning and I might as well keep going. So I changed course for Wick and was soon barrelling along with what became a force six up the bum. This was all well and good until, once I'd got a good way across I looked at the entry in the pilot book for Wick, which says *"do not attempt entry in easterly winds over force four with a swell running"*. This was a force six running straight into the harbour.

I managed to get the harbour office on the phone and asked if entry was likely to be a problem. The nice old lady at the other end of the phone told me that the Harbour Master was out and about but that she was sure it'd be OK and there was plenty of room *'so just come on in dear'*. I explained that it wasn't space in the harbour I was worried about, but being battered to death on the harbour wall by the massive breakers. She was momentarily confused but explained again that there was plenty of room and they didn't mind me coming in. She also explained that when she left at five p.m. she put the phone through to the Harbour Master's mobile. She did not explain why she couldn't put me through before five.

By five I had little choice – it was either Wick or another 50 miles to Kirkwall, so I took a chance on Wick. In the end it was OK and the Harbour Master talked me in, but I suspect it would have been difficult if the force six had been blowing for a day or two and created more swell. My worries were assuaged a bit by the fact that it was gloriously sunny all day. It may be irrational but you never feel you can come to much harm if it's nice and sunny.

There's a big new guest pontoon in Wick. Unfortunately it's in the outer harbour and subject to large amounts of surge and scend in even quite gentle conditions. A huge, substantial concrete affair the pontoon is apparently lifted out entirely over winter, when the whole harbour becomes untenable by any craft. Lovely.

Though it remained resolutely sunny, it was still early May and the evenings a tad chilly, so Zoph's charcoal stove came into its own. Started in Wick it ran continuously for a record three days and kept the chill off. Later Ian Cameron, a friend for Port Edgar and one of my crew for the North Sea crossing, expressed some nervousness at having a solid fuel stove on board, convinced of the certainty of carbon monoxide poisoning. It's amazing how many people, many of whom live in substantially wooden houses with soft furnishings, find the concept of a wood fire on a plastic boat difficult to come to terms with. Just to reassure those people, the stove itself is actually made of steel, not in fact wood.

Approaching Fair Isle

North to the Independent Republic of Shetland

Wick being, if anything, an even less appealing and more depressed town than Peterhead, I was glad that the forecast was good for the following day's passage to Kirkwall. Last time I went to Orkney I had thick fog all the way across the Pentland Firth into Scapa Flow. This time I took the easier and less fraught route in a big easterly arc, staying eight miles off the Pentland Skerries. That way you are well clear of the dodgy tides and dangerous seas. Again it was full sun, this time with a gentle south-easterly that allowed me to sail about half of the 50 miles. Once again, of course, there was fog right in the middle of the main shipping lanes, where ships from half of Europe batter through on their way across the Atlantic.

The AIS (Automatic Identification System) was as usual reassuring, showing all ships over 300 tonnes on the laptop chartplotter. I tried to put to the back of my mind the possibility of being mown down by a ship of less than 300 tonnes.

A day's rest in Kirkwall included a cycle on my folding Brompton bike across Orkney's South Mainland to one of the few churches in the world which is actually worth visiting for the emotional experience – the Italian chapel at Lamb Holm. Though just a couple of Nissan huts bolted together, this construction by Italian prisoners of war in the early '40s is actually quite moving.

Kirkwall has a fine posh marina with a few boats on passage. One such was 'Tarka of Lorne', a 40ft, flush decked Hallberg Rassy and probably the boat I would plump for if ever I traded up from Zoph.

Chatting to Tarka's skipper I discovered that they were also heading for the Lofotens, but direct from Shetland, not the long, wimpy way round like me. Mind you they were fully crewed. I wished them luck and joked that I'd probably see them there.

Hallberg Rassys are of course famously high quality Swedish cruising yachts. I'd recently read an article about Christoph Rassy, the elderly founder of the brand (Mr Hallberg ducked out early on), who was circumnavigating in his Hallberg Rassy 62. A 62 foot boat was a bit big even for my fantasy life, but perhaps one day I'd have a forty footer like Tarka.

I had thought I might leave Zoph in Kirkwall for a while, but of course the forecast continued to be for sun and light winds, boringly enough, so the next day I sailed the twenty miles to Stronsay in preparation for a couple of hops to Shetland.

When sailing in Orkney you always need to plan for the tides. Just for once, surprisingly, perfect timing seemed to demand leaving at about half nine in the morning to pick up the tide north out of Kirkwall. I would then arrive at the edge of Stronsay Firth at slack water and again pick up the tide to Stronsay. Not only was the timing right but with a force four easterly I sailed all the way, partly on a fine reach and partly close hauled. There were some very odd bits of choppy, swirly sea which gave a graphic inkling of what conditions could be like in strong winds and full spring tidal flows.

Stronsay has a single guest mooring between it and the nearby island of Papa Stronsay which, I was assured by the bloke in the shop, was both well maintained and free, so I picked it up. There were two small problems with this mooring – it was a hell of a row to the pub on Stronsay and a bit too close to Papa Stronsay, an island populated entirely by an eccentric brand of Christian monk most of whom, predictably, seem to be American. They had the habit (pun intended) of ringing the bloody church bells at god-forsaken hours of the morning, which would have woken someone who had not taken the precaution of consuming large quantities of alcohol in the pub.

Avoiding Monky Island I took the Brompton ashore and cycled half way across Stronsay and back. The green, pastoral landscape of Orkney is in stark contrast to the heather clad, uncultivated territory of the western isles. Presumably this is to do with the different land ownership pattern, the relative lack of major estates and the fact that, as far as I'm aware, the clearances never happened here. This means that many relatively small islands have what appear to be viable and economically active populations. It also means that most of the Orkney islands are spectacularly green. In the sun it was all bright green ground and bright blue sky, as artificial looking as a Microsoft screensaver.

At first sight it would appear that many of the economically active people are incomers. Stronsay's pub, shop and café are all run by English couples. All are twelve month a year operations and none are particularly aimed at tourists. They are just operating local businesses and keeping the place going. There's various brands of English incomers in rural Scotland, some of whom on parts of the west coast are not exactly adding anything – absentee landlords and holiday home owners driving property prices up – but as an Englishman who has lived in Scotland for 30 years it seemed to me that the incomers to Stronsay were a wholly positive influence.

I was pondering this as I cycled along and became aware of a traffic jam building up behind me, albeit only one car long. Stronsay is only seven miles across, so if you drive at more than twenty miles an hour the experience is soon over. People seemed to enjoy crawling long behind me at seven knots on a two lane road, waiting for the island's longest straight to open up so they could zoom past at a heart-stopping fifteen knots. It passed a bit of time and they could imagine they were in a five mile tailback into work on a Monday morning. A bit of nostalgia for the incomers.

Practically everyone I saw here – and on Mainland Orkney – waved at me as they passed. I assume that, even if they don't recognise you, they think they

The Harbour on Fair Isle

probably ought to, so wave just to be on the safe side so you don't think they are rude. Very nice anyway.

The forecast, of course, was OK for the 42 mile hop to Fair Isle. Perfect weather but not quite a perfect breeze this time, with a north-easterly force three to four on the nose. Still, there wasn't a lot of sea running and the motor-sail in the sun was pleasant enough. As I approached Fair Isle from the south I saw a sail approaching from the North and accelerated to grab the best spot, not knowing how much room there was. As I did so the other boat dropped sail and appeared to do the same. This other boat turned out to be a 32ft catamaran which had tried crossing to Norway but given up half way when they heard the forecast of contrary winds.

The little harbour on Fair Isle is an idyllic wee place and pretty sheltered given that it's on a speck in the north Atlantic. It is a bit subject to swell from the north-east, which was exactly where the wind was, of course. However a new mole (why are lumps of rubble dumped in the sea called moles?) gave a bit of extra shelter so it was fine. It was all very cosmopolitan in the harbour, with a Norwegian boat and a Swedish one, as well as the cat and 'Boomerang', a Port Edgar boat just completing a whistle-stop tour to Bergen and returning to Port Ed. Impressive going for so early in the year, it being only May 13th. It was, I suppose, appropriate that Boomerang was coming back so promptly.

I was about to raft up on Boomerang when a bloke in a wee open boat zoomed over and said that I could raft up on the Fair Isle ferry, the 'Good Shepherd', since it wasn't going anywhere for the next day or two. So I had my own massive steel pontoon and a door opening onto the deck of the ferry from my cockpit. Such a thing would be unthinkable on the west of Scotland where the execrable Cal Mac rule the waves and monopolise the harbours. A nice friendly start.

Fair Isle is famous for its bird life but is actually quite pastoral and – at least in May's gorgeous weather, civilised and benign. Physically it reflects it's position half way between Orkney and Shetland. The northern half – nearest Shetland – is wild, heather clad and rocky. The southern half – nearest Orkney – is farmed, green and pastoral, dotted with houses. All in all a very pleasant environment and I Brompted from one end to the other.

As I wandered around, Gordon McEquinox phoned and said he'd pencilled me in as crew to cross the Atlantic in the ARC (Atlantic Rally for Cruisers) on

Equinox in November and December. Once I got back from my 3000 mile trip to Lofoten I had another 3000 mile trip to look forward to.

Fair Isle is half way between Stronsay and Lerwick and there being no particular tidal gates I left at 9.30 for Shetland's capital. With a force three north-westerly we had a good sail for a while, but then the wind backed and headed us so the motor went on. One Norwegian yacht sailed past heading south. Sumburgh has a reputation for dodgy seas in some conditions but today it was benign.

I realised that the last time I had seen the lighthouse at Sumburgh was two days after my eighteenth birthday in 1975. When flying to Shetland I looked upwards (yes upwards) through the plane window in a break in the thick fog and saw the lighthouse looming very near. I often wondered if we nearly hit the bloody thing as the pilot banked steeply round it and hoped nobody on board had noticed. I flew there then to take my first ever job, labouring for the summer with the company that dug all the holes for the Sullom Voe oil terminal. At its peak constructing Sullom Voe employed 5000 people, but in 1975 it was just 150 Irish blokes and me and my mate Dave. What a baptism of fire that was. We only worked a 79.5 hour week, the Irish lads did 89.5 hours, four weeks on one week off. Me and Dave got no days off as we worked seven days a week for three months. That summer taught me how to smoke 40 roll-ups a day and drink 10 pints a night, which was something of a mixed blessing.

Thirty three years later and near the end of the life of Sullom Voe oil terminal there was a fair amount of oil-related shipping traffic around busy Lerwick harbour, where I saw my first clouds for ten days. Arriving on the visitors' pontoon I tied up behind a couple of Norwegian yachts in town for the booze. There would seem to be a lot more Scandinavian boats in Shetland than visiting ones from elsewhere in the UK.

By the time I reached Lerwick I'd done 345 miles in eight trips over nine days. A fair old way really and averaging 43 miles a day.

The Shetlanders famously claim close kinship with the Norwegians. I can only presume that the tall, blond, tanned Shetlanders are all indoors every time I hit the streets, since none of them were in evidence. Pink, overweight, fleshy and quintessentially British ones yes, but none of the ones of overtly Scandinavian stock.

Lerwick seems basically to be run by a bloke called Bert. His principal source of income seems to be selling booze to Norwegians. His modus

Leaving Fair Isle

operandi is to appear in a van at the guest pontoon in the harbour and enquire whether you might be leaving the European Union. If you reply shiftily that you might possibly be heading for Norway, he offers to fill your boat to the gunwales with duty free booze and fags. And this is not your old fashioned 20% off airport duty free. I'm talking a pound a packet for fags and whisky at £3.50 a litre. Suitably loaded up you then head off into the sunset promising that yes, honestly, you are going to Norway, honest. You might, of course, if you were of a dishonest bent, simply nip back home to Port Edgar or somewhere with a year's supply of cheap hooch, but I know you're a law abiding citizen.

Even if you do go to Norway – and the large majority of Bert's customers are Norwegian – there is absolutely no correlation between the amount of 'duty free' he will sell and the amount Norwegians are allowed to import. Incredibly, this fantastic dodge seems to be legal, at least at the UK end.

When I was there four Norwegian lads in a scruffy yacht had arrived from Bergen at six am. At midday they started drinking. They woke me with loud music at 6.30 the next morning. They finally hit the sack about 7.30 am after boozing for a solid nineteen and a half hours. At one p.m. the same day they sailed back to Norway. Happily they wouldn't have been hung over. They would still have been absolutely pissed.

I had enquired about a marina berth to leave Zoph for a couple of weeks and of course the man in charge of Gremista Marina was Bert. He gave me a U-shaped pontoon designed for a 45 footer in a perfectly sheltered marina filled with privately owned berths. The price? £15 a week. Not per day, per week. Gremista marina is not the most lovely of spots - right next to the power station. But at £15 a week it's quite possibly the world's cheapest marina.

I wandered to the ferry port to buy a ticket to Aberdeen on the very plush, comfortable, practically empty and reasonably priced ferry.

"What do you mean I need a passport to get on the ferry?! I thought Shetland was part of the UK. It's just more evidence of the bleedin' police state!" I complained to the woman at the ticket desk. I was however grateful for the spur of the moment decision I had made ten days earlier to stick my passport in my back pocket on the way down to Port Ed. Though I hadn't been heading abroad I thought I might as well put the passport on board ready for the trip to Norway. It's easy to forget your travel documents when travelling by boat, because nobody ever asks for them. Had I not done so, I would be stuck on Shetland for life.

Shetland is now effectively the only place you need a passport to travel to within the UK, unless you travel on your own boat. The ferry company demands photo ID on the grounds that, apparently, people have been suspected to be travelling under false names. *"What if I want to travel under a false name? Why shouldn't I?"* I demanded petulantly of the check-in woman as security guards shifted about nervously and began eyeing me up for a strip search and a spot of anal probing. They couldn't tell me what criteria they were using to decide what was an acceptable name and what they would do to people with unacceptable names. Presumably the private company that runs the ferry would deny them access to this part of our fair country, or stop them leaving.

So if there's anyone out there with a name deemed unacceptable for travel to Shetland, just let me know and I'll try to arrange to run you up there next summer on Zoph.

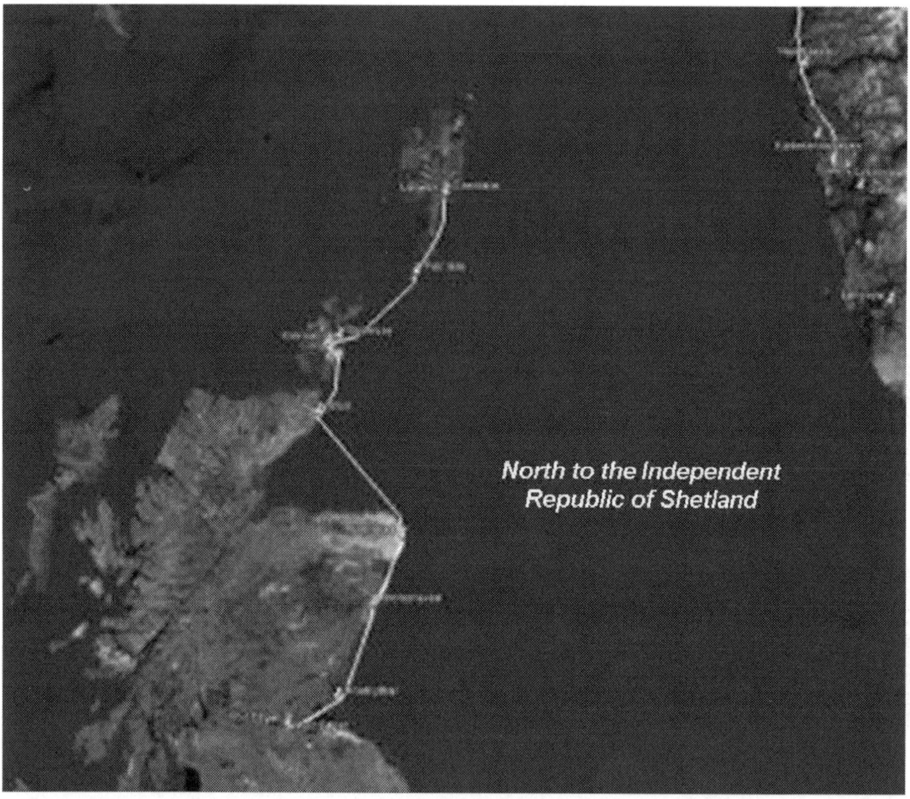

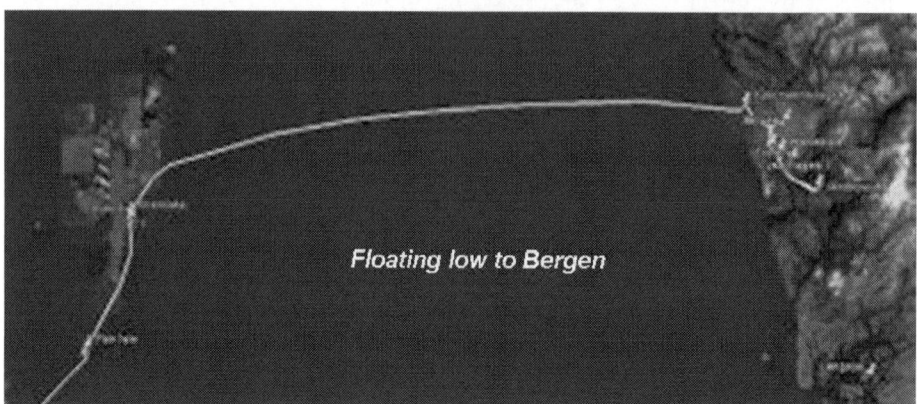

North to the Independent Republic of Shetland

Floating low to Bergen

Floating Low to Bergen

Having sorted out a crew for the North Sea crossing back in Edinburgh (Ian Cameron of the Dufour 25 'Psyche' and another friend from Port Edgar, Fiona Harrison of the Sadler 32 'Moonwhite') and anxiously scanned the forecasts for nearly two weeks, I returned to Shetland on the self-same ferry, clutching my passport in an angrily clenched fist. The forecast looked to be set fair for the next two or three days, with a respite in the constant easterlies which Sod's law had ensured we had all spring and early summer. I was anxious to leave for Bergen as quickly as possible while the weather held.

Back at Gremista marina Bert tried to charge me only £15, believing I'd only been in the marina for one week. In a rare bout of honesty I gave him the full £30 for two weeks as I took delivery of a small booze top-up amounting to no more than 40 or 50 litres of beer and whisky in the main town visitor harbour.

The boat club bar seems to be just about the only decent pub in Lerwick and has good showers. Like a lot of places round the harbour, the signs are all in English and Norwegian – an indication of the connections – albeit perhaps not genetic – between Shetland and Norway. With the recent demise of the ferry from Rosyth on the Fort to Zeebrugge, the seasonal ferry between Lerwick and Bergen is, I believe, the only direct passenger sea link between Scotland and mainland Europe. It is telling that it doesn't even depart from mainland Scotland.

Ian arrived on the morning ferry from Aberdeen and we paced the dockside waiting for Fiona, who was flying in (on an aeroplane, not under her own steam). We barely gave her time to get one foot on the toe rail before we cast off and headed out into a rather dreich North Sea with a force 3 on the nose. We motored past Out Skerries, a small set of islands with a good natural harbour. We headed out in a northerly curve towards Bergen. The wind was forecast to come back from the north at possibly up to a force 6, with the stronger winds to the south, so it made sense to put in as much northing as we could.

As we motorsailed towards Out Skerries - fully crewed for once - and Zoph dug her stern in as I opened the throttle, we noticed that there was a good 6 inches of water in the 'self-draining' – or in this instance self-filling – cockpit. She was certainly floating well below the official waterline. I suggested that this might have something to do with the number of pies consumed by the crew over the years. The crew, in their turn, pointed out that it might have something to do with the 450 cans and 250 bottles of beer, 40 litres of spirits and 30 bottles of wine on board. Laughing hysterically at the idea that we should jettison some of these bare essential supplies, I considered briefly what we could get rid of. Perhaps all the water, a spare anchor or one of the crew.

But no, wet though it was in the cockpit, she was still floating with plenty of freeboard. Donning wellies we continued on our way, *'floating low to Lofoten'*, I thought. Bugger. As soon as I'd hit on the title I knew that now I was committed. There'd be no swanning about in southern Norway for weeks for me. Now I had to make it up well beyond the Arctic Circle to Lofoten so that I could legitimately use the title.

Most of the way across to Bergen we got some push from the sails but though we did turn the engine off for a fine reach in a force four the next morning, the breeze died after a couple of hours and the engine, I'm afraid, went back on. All in all it was a pretty easy and unremarkable crossing. Just as the previous year, the weather went from Scottish dreich to Nordic niceness, but this time we were followed during our last few hours by lowering dark clouds and thunder. All very portentous and always worrying when you are essentially clinging to the only big metal stick for miles around jutting out of the water. Ian gave us his physics teacher lecture on lightning science and boats.

We added a few miles with my northerly curve, but negotiated a narrow channel in behind the islands on the outer approach to Bergen. I had intended to press on to the proper big harbour at Bergen, where we would have arrived at about three a.m. But I was forgetting that this was Norway. In Norway everyone has a boat and every village has a perfectly sheltered harbour. So when we saw the lights of a village a couple of hundred yards in from the exposed sea we just headed for them. We picked our way down the narrow channel into the small, deep harbour, tied up to a wall in an uncharted village that turned out to be called Kjobmannsvagen and cracked open some beers. It was twenty to midnight on May 31st, twenty minutes before June. We'd done 195 miles in exactly 34 hours, to the minute, from Lerwick.

Happily both were able to stay on for a few days and experience a wee bit of idyllic Nordic cruising. The previous year my crew had to fly pretty much straight back, so got to experience the fraught, difficult bit but not the fun holiday bit.

We woke the next day to glorious full sun and Fiona woke to a slight hangover I think (she's a bit of a lightweight when it comes to beer, if truth be told). The sun stayed, with a brief four hour period of twilight every day, for the next 8 days. Fiona's hangover, happily, didn't.

We had a nice gentle motor down behind the sheltering islands to Bergen, the crew suitably appreciative of the

fantastic cruising environment and Fiona plotting how to skive off work all summer and get Moonwhite across the North Sea next year.

Rafting up in the centre of Bergen against a Norwegian 40 footer with two French blokes on it, we were soon rafted upon in our turn by a speed boat with a fantastically pissed crew. The holiday atmosphere was palpable and the number of '*Kiss*' tee shirts was quite alarming. Apparently 20,000 people were to attend a Kiss concert that night and most of them seemed to have chosen speed boats as their preferred mode of transport. Presumably the further outposts of Scandinavia are the last places on earth where tired old rockers like Kiss can find an audience. One imagines that the more rural bits of Norway might have more than their fair share of head-bangers.

But though we were promised uncompromising partying until dawn and people did get proper fall-over drunk, this was after all Scandinavia. All the crowds dissipated quite meekly and suddenly at exactly 1 am. The crowds snaked back through town and everyone went home to bed in their speedboat or, exceptionally, their house.

After a day's sightseeing round Bergen and a trip on the funicular railway to see the spectacular view, we had a gentle sail and a motorsail down to the island of Tyssoy, to give Ian and Fiona a taste of Nordic fore-and-aft mooring. Astonishingly, I managed to deposit the stern anchor in about the right place and bring the bow in to a rock without hitting it, allowing Ian to hop ashore on Edge's patented Bow-Plank. All this was done without undue shouting or cock-ups. Much, much more by luck than judgement.

British boat builders are the only ones in the world who never envisage anyone hopping on and off the boat over the bow. They therefore manufacture pulpits which curve all the way round the bow, effectively preventing anyone from boarding there. This is a hopeless arrangement for practically everywhere outside Britain. Hence Edge's patented plank arrangement, consisting of a makeshift and temporary bowsprit made of a plank of wood from B&Q. Stylish.

All the other boats in the anchorage – three or four motorboats – upped anchor and left before sunset. Speaking to the skipper of one it seems that, given suitable weather, they do all just leave work in Bergen around four, hop into their boats and spend six hours or so in any one of a choice of hundreds of idyllic anchorages, all less than half an hour from their homes. They do this on every decent weekday of the summer and it's a tradition that goes back generations.

They've got something right about their summer lifestyles, these Norgians.

Left alone in this calm anchorage, more perfectly sheltered than anything in Scotland, we had a wander the length and breadth of the little island. Which of course, being half a mile long, has a commuter village on it and a series of bridges linking it to the mainland.

Next morning we put in at Hjellestad Båthavn, our port of arrival in Norway the previous year, so that Fiona could sort out a taxi and stuff for the airport the following morning. Norway seems to be full of Båthavns and it's nice to see the Norwegians providing so many havens for their flying mammals.

Fiona felt a bit rough that first morning in Norway

After an hour or two we sailed and motored to Lyssoy Island, where we anchored in the most sheltered pool imaginable. A hundred yards across, with a flat bottom five metres deep and an entry about ten metres wide and two metres deep. It's sometimes hard to believe that these places just occur naturally in Norway.

After dinner I decided on a swim, since a load of sprogs were diving in off a boat nearby. Teacher Ian became very teacherly indeed, with dire warnings about the certain death that would ensue if you dived in the pool within three hours of eating. I'm afraid I ignored him however and, though undoubtedly cold, it wasn't the shock to the system that diving into Scotland's perishing seas usually produces, especially as early in the summer as June the second. In fact I'd almost say it was quite pleasant, though brief. By August the water in these sheltered pools gets positively tepid and I recorded sea temperatures of up to 20°C.

Fiona needed to be away frighteningly early in the morning, so in the evening we motored – with just a little sailing – back to the marina at Hyellestad. She nearly avoided waking me as she left at about four a.m. and I grumpily nodded off again for another six hours or so.

Ian was staying another couple of days, so we took a side trip, sailing ever so slowly the twenty miles or so down to Godoysund, where a defunct hotel provided pontoons and there were fifty or sixty sheltered, tree

Bergen. The View from the Top

The landscape north of Bergen

lined bays providing yet more perfect anchorages. We sailed under jib at one knot up the canal-like passages between wee islands. We finally settled on a spot where we could drop a stern anchor and tie the bow to a tree, then take another line from the stern ashore to a tree on the other side of the bay. So attached we could happily have ridden out a hurricane.

There wasn't a hurricane however and therein lay a small problem – we were slightly beset by midges. I'd been going on about how jammy the Norwegians were 'cos they didn't have midges, but undoubtedly there were a few in Godoysund. Not anything like in proper Scottish west coast numbers, but a few nonetheless.

I proposed going ashore and blew up the Avon Redcrest dinghy. Ian was very dubious about boarding it and gave me quite a long physics teacher lecture about air pressure. To summarise, we'd certainly die if he ever attempted to board the dinghy again. I therefore left him on board and went for a row around the lovely creeks and islands.

The following day was another phew what a scorcher and Ian's last. We sailed and motored and motorsailed in flat calm waters under a baking sun back towards Hjellestad, poking into a couple of perfect anchorages just to have a look, but not stopping. Often, perversely, the best wee breezes seemed to be around and coming off the land, whilst the more open stretches of sea were particularly glassy. A couple of racing yachts were out for a spin. It must be a particularly frustrating part of the world to race round the cans in and one in which I imagine local knowledge generally wins through.

The next morning – or rather that night – Ian left at the same time as Fiona had. Needless to say I selflessly didn't shift from my pit to see him off.

Godoysund

The Way North

Now I knew that the proper travelling part of the north-bound Norwegian leg of my journey had to begin. Though I had all summer, it's a bugger of a way up the coast of Norway and I had to put in a decent average day's passage. The forecast was set fair for another three days, then the long period of beautiful settled, sunny weather the Norges had been enjoying was due to break. The most famously dangerous bit of the Norwegian coast – the headland at Stad – was 150 miles away. I decided to put in two or three largish passages – well, largish for me motoring solo up tortuous twisting channels – and race the weather.

I remained unconvinced, by the way, by Norwegian claims of dangerous headlands and particularly dodgy bits of water. The fact is that the large majority of the coast of Norway is fantastically sheltered by the string of islands designed, Douglas Adams tells us, by Slartibartfast to protect the motor-boating hordes. Most Norwegians zip about in the seagoing equivalent of a Ford Focus in these sheltered waters. So as soon as there's a bit where they actually have to go into the open sea the Norwegian Hydrographic Service stamps 'Dangerous Waves' all over the charts and an 'escort service' is provided for small boats. Presumably those ones that can't get dates for themselves. Bring a Norwegian over to Scotland and stick him in the Corryvrechan or the Pentland Firth and he'll soon learn what dangerous water is.

From Hjellestad I went 57 miles to the predictably fantastic natural harbour of Hardbakke, via Bergen, the Radfjord and Sognesjøen. Since there was no wind and I had to motor I thought I might as well take the inshore – or inland – route.

It's a perverse and unlikely fact that there

Norwegians can squeeze in major industrial installations just about anywhere

Bergen's often brand new ancient and historical buildings

Approaching the harbour at Hardbakke

are apparently very few fjords in Norway. At least not many worth taking a boat up. A fjord is, of course, an inlet of the sea. Taking a quick look at a small scale chart of the Norwegian coast would suggest that there's fjords everywhere. A closer look at a large scale chart, however, reveals that, in fact, most of these apparent inlets actually pass right through a chunk of Norway to create islands. Further inland there are of course, dead ends. These are, however, often many tens of miles inland from the open sea, surrounded by mountains and with fickle winds. There's very little reason to travel up them in a slow boat.

Reading the charts – or rather the chart plotter – is like reading a road map for some of these channels. Looked at on a small scale you'd swear there was just land. Then you zoom in and see bits of water. Zoom in a lot more and you realise they are all connected channels between islands. In Scotland we are used to lochs stopping at the end. In Norway most of them don't. They just keep going right on through. But though the channels are narrow they aren't that difficult to pilot your way through. Most of them are well marked with the simple buoyage system that runs from south to north. The most common mark is a steel stick with a green or red mark and a metal 'flag' letting you know which side of it to pass. In the most inland channels these are really just like road markings and the channels are easy to follow.

So Zoph headed north up a series of intricate 'sounds', as opposed to fjords. I motored up channels not shown at all on the Admiralty 1:50,000 charts. Across Fensfjord, up Anneland Sundet, across Sognesjøen and into Indre-Steinsund. Occasionally with a little help from the jib but mostly under motor.

Zoph is fitted with a wind vane self steering system (called Leo for hopefully obvious reasons) which is great in the right context but hopeless in windless conditions and up tortuous channels. The previous year my tiller-pilot, mercifully, broke and I bought a new one, called Techno-Leo. What a revelation a half-decent tiller-pilot was! Ideal for cooking your three course dinner whilst motoring up narrow glassy sounds.

Ian had used the *phrase 'cute overload'* to describe the landscape around Bergen and the scenery, tweenery and wee buildings on the way to Hardbakke were

Heading north

indeed massively, almost painfully twee. Apparently *'cute overload'* is a web site dedicated to the extraordinarily twee. I didn't dwell too much on why Ian frequented it.

I tied up for free on a private pontoon just outside a pub in a harbour again more perfect than any natural harbour in Britain, secure against a hurricane from any direction and pictureskew to boot.

Next day there was actually a bit of wind at times. A harbinger of the break in the weather that was expected. At times it was up to twenty knots apparent. At other times it was down to bugger all. By and large it came from the north west, but it couldn't really make up its mind where it wanted to come from. It increased as I skirted the approaches to the town of Florø and the engine actually went off for a while. However the wind often headed us and the jib was furled and unfurled about five times.

I had a fast motorsail down Frøysjøen but then met a two to three knot contrary tide as we turned north-west towards Måløy. Strong tide was not something I was used to in Norway. I would have to face the fact that as I went further north the tides got a bit more Scottish in strength and height. Happily, you have to go as far as the North Cape and well over 70° north before the tides become as ferocious or as high or the landscape gets as bleak, treeless and unpopulated as most of the west of Scotland.

Another phenomenon I wasn't used to in Norway and thought I had escaped for the summer was fog. Often it looks rather aesthetic from a distance and it looked beautiful as it rolled in from the sea up the high sided fjords. It billowed in pure white rolls between the dramatic cliffs that formed the entrance to Måløy. As it swept majestically in from the sea I swept rather less majestically towards Måløy from the landward side, having taken the inside track up the coast. Unfortunately the fog won the race and soon it looked rather less aesthetically pleasing since I was in the middle of thick, damp fog feeling my way towards a strange port up narrow channels. But Måløy was on a side shoot of the main fjord leading inland and as soon as I turned up it the fog cleared to pure sunshine again. Apparently the fog, being mere water vapour, didn't have the wit to pursue me up the side channel and I lost it and tied up – after a 62 mile trip - in the almost deserted but quite substantial guest harbour of Måløy. Måløy is a relatively unprepossessing place. There's nothing dreadful about it but you felt it had probably seen better days. In many ways, let's face it, it felt a bit more like a small town in Britain. Listless youth hung about in quiet streets wondering whether it was time for Norwegians to take up petty vandalism or graffiti.

The next day was the biggie. The fabled headland of Stad was just around the corner. The pilot book, more tour guide than useful passage planner, doesn't bother to give directions to pass Stadlandet, but does say that it *'sticks out like an angrily clenched fist'*. Which was reassuring.

Passing Floro

Approaching fog banks near Maloy

The forecast looked good for the first part of the day, with increasing south-westerlies later. South west was an apparently good wind direction for me heading north, but Norwegians all swear that south westerlies are the worst for sea conditions. I expect it's to do with all that stuff about convergence, divergence and the coriolis effect that us sailors are supposed to know about. I motorsailed out to the peninsula of Stadlandet, but once there the motor went off and Zoph was under full sail at between five and eight knots with a force five to six up the chuff.

I had intended to scuttle in behind Stad and find shelter nearby, but given the fast passage speed I decided to carry on to Ålesund. This may have been a bad decision since at one p.m. it started pissing down. The high that had dominated for the past month and given Norway a rare scorcher had finally been shoved out of the way by depressions. However I made it to Ålesund, albeit soaked to the skin.

I own some mid-range Gill waterproofs, which are notable for the fact that they aren't in the least bit waterproof. Probably the most expensive offshore gear is waterproof and the cheapest bright orange plastic fisherman's stuff certainly is. The problem with the mid range stuff is that they make it out of a material that's nice and soft and matt, so that it looks like the expensive stuff. They need to cut costs however and do so by using material that isn't even vaguely waterproof. The Gill gear went into the locker for the rest of the summer and out came the nine quid Millets plastic mac.

Anyway, the passage was fifty four miles mostly sailed at an average passage speed of 6.4 knots, which is almost exactly Zoph's hull speed.

On the pontoons at Ålesund it felt like a real cruising community. I rafted up on a Norgian Bavaria, but there were Germen, Dutch and Swedes in. Only six or seven yachts but all heading north like me. As always Zoph was by far the smallest cruising yacht in the harbour. My eyes began to scale boats down and see forty footers

Fog rolling through from the Atlantic

as pretty wee boats. After a while in Norway I would occasionally see something a bit smaller and think 'gosh that's a tiny yacht', then realise that it was six feet longer than my boat.

Ålesund is apparently famously Germanic looking and not like other Norwegian towns. It burned down at the start of the twentieth century and was rebuilt to designs by a load of architects from Germany and elsewhere. For some reason, according to my guide book 'Kaiser Wilhelm footed the bill'. Of course you need to be familiar with lots of other Norwegian towns before you can be suitably surprised by one that doesn't look like the others and I was insufficiently experienced to be amazed, but it's a pleasant place to wander in. Its greatest annoyance that day was a sprog off one of the motor cruisers who spent the entire day razzing round and round the harbour in a little inflatable with a noisy outboard. This was to become a recurrent theme in many harbours, but murder was nearly done that day.

The next dodgy bit of coast – the 'Hustadvika' – was only 40 miles or so away but I decided to stop before it for the night to gather my resources. I left Ålesund in a south westerly force three which rapidly increased to a wet and squally force six. The trouble with increasing winds on a broad reach or run is that you need to come into the wind to put in a reef. At first you think there's not really too much wind, only in the gusts. By the time you've decided there is too much wind, the prospect of turning into to tuck in a couple of reefs it becomes an unpleasant one, so you carry on. The other problem with a dead run is that the jib doesn't fill well and tends to snap and thrash about. Unpleasant and not good for the rig. However with the jib furled and under main only it was a reasonable sail.

I gave up my ambition of sailing to

The Fart Dampener. A common Norwegian anal suppression device not yet available in the rest of Europe

the outlying small island of Ona – which I only wanted to do so that I could send Anna a text reading 'amonona' – and threaded through the rocks to the island of Finnoy, with a harbour entrance tortuous even by Norwegian standards. I negotiated my way through he rocky islets on the southern approach to the harbour in the swirling seas with a good force six

blowing. I did at least two 180 degree turns to get in. Zoph was the only boat on the hundred metre long pontoon in a harbour so incredibly sheltered you could use the water as a shaving mirror in a hurricane. The Norgian pilot book I had borrowed from some chums at Port Ed describes it as a 'duck pond'. The 'E-book' pilot however says that "A first time visit is best done in settled weather and with caution". I was quite pleased that I'd not noticed that beforehand.

Finnoy is half way between Shetland and the Arctic. It's a square mile of island at the edge of the North Atlantic. Its west coast looks a bit like the Hebrides – low machar and rocks – In its east and centre the trees grow straight and tall. There are lush crops in all the fields. There are suburbs, shops and industry. Stuff which we are told is impossible on the west of Scotland at 55°N happens here at 63°N. I was to discover that this pattern of lush agriculture, suburbs and tall trees continues a lot further north, way above the Arctic Circle. Yet we still remain convinced that the Mull of Kintyre is too northern, bleak and isolated to grow anything or have an effective economy.

These Norwegians are a spoiled bunch. In the harbour were two huge floating wooden sheds – boathouses really – moored to the banks. Inside one a large gin palace floated. In the other a sailing dinghy with its mast up and... get this... its sails set! Nobody about. Presumably its owner just couldn't be bothered taking the sails down, so built a floating aircraft hangar for his dinghy. Just sailed out of the shed and back into the shed when he'd finished.

Though a damp evening I cycled to the next island, Harøya. Nearly all Norwegian Islands are of course linked by causeways and bridges involving serious civil engineering and the shifting of vast quantities of rock. I'd

Alesund

guess the average is about 10,000 tonnes of rock per inhabitant. In the wet fishing harbour there was a big steel German yacht from Rendsberg, in the Kiel canal, where I had left Zoph for a fortnight the year before. I approached the single occupant and explained this and we had a brief chat. This was later to prove to be something of a mistake. He was heading north as fast as possible, he said, aiming at the North Cape, before turning for home in mid July.

Back on Zoph the next morning it continued raining and another dramatic sea rescue was in the offing. The thirty knot winds of the night had abated a bit to twenty knots. I had just made a final decision not to shift at all that day when all of a sudden the rain stopped, the wind went down to a nice force three, the clouds blew away and we had a hot, sunny, calm day. Of course my final decision was reversed and I headed off. I decided on just a wee side trip, since I wasn't prepared for the Hustadvika, it was getting late in the day and we were due more strong winds that evening.

I'd only sailed about four miles when I saw a small boat bobbing about off the port bow. Most Norwegians seem to spend the best part of their lives floating about in wee boats dangling a fishing line, so this seemed unremarkable. A casual squint through the binoculars however revealed that it was a jet-ski – or 'personal watercraft' as I believe they are supposed to be called. (Why they are more personal than, say, a canoe, I don't know). What's more, it was a jet ski bobbing about on open sea with nobody on board. I motored over to take a look. There was certainly nobody about. Rather foolishly I called 'hello', as if a tiny person was likely to appear from under the seat. Clearly there were three possibilities. The jet ski might have broken loose in last night's gale and floated here. Its owner might have come off it and drowned in the cold sea. Or some public spirited person might have nicked it and set it adrift to rid the world of one more annoying source of noise pollution.

Clearly I had to bear in mind the second possibility and inform someone of my find. The most obvious route was to call up on the VHF on channel sixteen. This I tried to do again and again. But calling the Coastguard in Norway is a dead loss. I later discovered that the people on the other end of the ether are just called 'radio'. So it might

Bud sunset

be 'Bergen Radio', or 'Trondheim Radio' you need to call. Unfortunately they respond only to their exact title, so if you don't know whose area you are in or what exactly they are known as you can call until you are blue in the face and you'll get no answer.

The next option was phoning the Coastguard. I couldn't find a number of course, so opted for my usual solution of phoning Anna and getting her to look it up on the internet. The web was however devoid of any mention of Norwegian Coastguard in English.

I finally took the 999 option, which seemed a bit extreme in the circumstances but appeared to work. I got through to a slightly nonplussed emergency services telephone bloke who asked for my call sign, which I even managed to remember in the proper language - *'Mike Whisky Hotel Bravo Seven'* - and promised to pass my message on.

Soon *'bleughbleugh radio'*, as the chap appeared to call himself, was calling me up on channel sixteen. If someone calls you up on 16 with your call sign, how do you respond? I responded with the boat's name, which the bloke completely ignored. After a few goes however we established communication.

I then made a total arse of reading out the jet-ski's registration number, completely forgetting the names for letters of the alphabet. Anyway, pretty soon a big lifeboat rib thingy appeared over the horizon and took the jet-ski in tow. They seemed largely unconcerned and of the opinion it had just broken free in last night's gales. Presumably a registration number is handy for this as you can quickly contact the owner and establish if he's drowned. Had I not called them up, of course, I'd have forever been convinced that someone had drowned, so the whole proceedings at least had the effect of assuaging my conscience, even though, on the negative side, they preserved a jet-ski.

Somewhat reassured I continued on, via a couple of anchorages to check them out, to the small, heavily treed island of Furoya, quite deep down an actual

The world's laziest dinghy sailor?

fjord. I had more or less decided on a spot where I could drop a stern anchor and tie to a rock when I rounded a corner and found, of course, an empty, brand new 100m long pontoon in a perfectly sheltered bay, with picnic tables ashore and enough room for at least 50 boats to

moor fore and aft. I tied Zoph
firmly and obsessively to a wee
perpendicular offshoot of the
pontoon ready for the night's
predicted gale, which happened
but which I scarcely noticed as we
rode it out alone in this perfect
shelter.

Travelling by ferry can be dangerous passing Bud: big guns trained on the Hurtigrute ship

The previous year the furthest
point of my cruise – that is the
greatest straight line distance
from Port Ed - had been about 515 miles, at the east end of Orust Island. At
Furoya we had broken this record. Port Ed was 522 miles away.

The oddly named but quite cute town of Bud is the last point before the
feared Hustadvika and the next day I had a gentle pootle there under motor via
a few more perfect anchorages and harbours. The guest pontoon near the
harbour entrance in the fishing port of Bud is said by the pilot book to be
'subject to swell'. Wick is subject to swell. Bud is subject to ripples. Any
anchorage in which you might notice at all that your boat is actually floating, as
opposed to set in concrete, is considered in Norway to be dangerously subject to
swell. I suspect many Norwegians, tied up in Port Ed at certain states of tide
with an easterly force six blowing would be subject to heart failure.

Later a couple of Norgian Bavarias came in crewed by glaikit young couples.
They appeared to be rolling quite a bit on the approach from the open sea and
they did say there had been a three metre swell after the strong westerlies of the
past couple of nights. They had taken the route outside the Hustadvika. I hoped
that by the following day the swell would have subsided sufficiently and I
would take the rock-dodging inside route. This involved incredibly intricate
pilotage between half submerged rocks with the swell breaking all over the
place, then an open sea passage, then more intricate rock dodging, this time in
calmer waters sheltered by skerries.

I plotted a route on the computerised chart. It had 35 turning points. My
Admiralty 1:50,000 chart was not nearly good enough to guide me through the
Hustadvika's inner route. Basically my life was in the hands of a slightly dodgy
laptop prone to crashing and Bill Gates' software. Not a situation I relished.

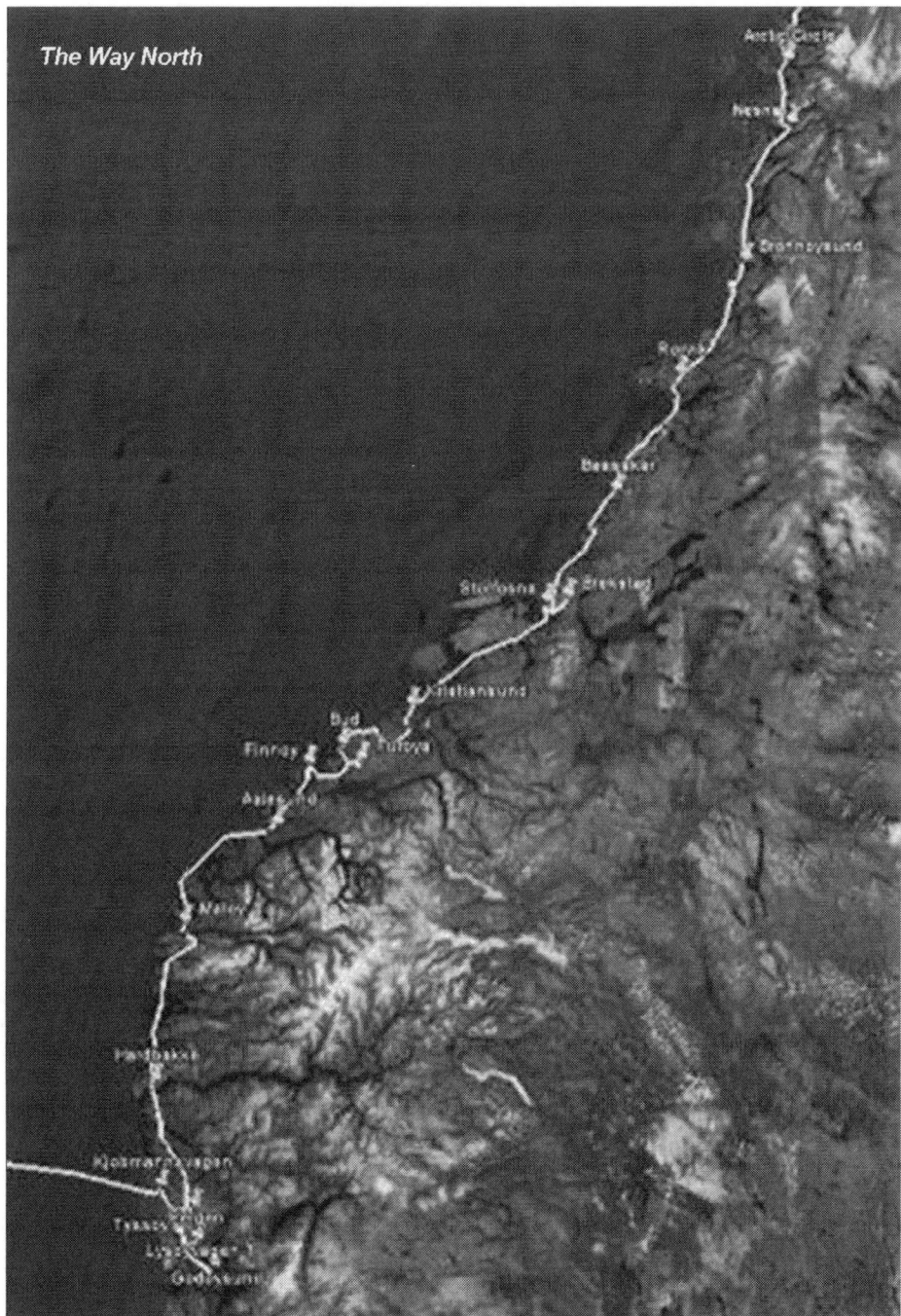

The Atlantic Backstreets

In the morning I headed out into the two metre swell rolling through the first gap between the rocks with just the main up with two reefs in it. Not that I was expecting much wind but I wanted to stop the rolling and be well under control amongst the rocks. There was spray coming off concealed rocks all over the place. I was up and down to the chart plotter every minute or so and trying to keep a line on the paper chart in case the bloody thing crashed – which it often does - or – as has also happened – the cheap GPS linked to the computer threw a wobbly. As it turned out the passage wasn't too bad, but only because the computer didn't crash.

After the open sea bit I threaded Zoph into perfectly sheltered pools which, once you were in them, you'd swear were completely land-locked with no way out. But there was always a route through. At one mark I almost decided that the buoyage was going in the wrong direction (it almost always goes from south to north in Norway). A greenish stick wanted me to leave it to starboard. But there was a rock directly to port of the stick. It turned out to be correct. You just had to thread your way down the five metre wide space between the stick and the rock.

Of course the Norwegians had built houses and boathouses and harbours around practically every little hole in the rocks. Every skerry over fifty metres or so across had a building of some sort on it.

When the Hustadvika spat Zoph out I passed under a 23m high bridge carrying what's called the 'Atlantic Road'. There are bridges and causeways linking seventeen islands and making the back route to Kristiansund up Lauvoyfjord and Kvernerfjord almost completely landlocked. I had a surprisingly good breeze at times in the flat calm sea of these Atlantic Backstreets surrounded by mountains and completed most of the rest of the trip under full sail with the odd bit of motoring. In the end doing better than six knots on a reach

Which side of the stick is this main shipping channel?

Kristiansund is a busy harbour with loads of local boats, but the only other sailing boat on the visitors' pontoon was the German I'd met in Finnoy. We engaged in a chat about those crazy Norwegians and how they build houses absolutely everywhere. Then he vouchsafed the view that Florø, for

The Atlantic Road

example, was filled with Pakistanis, that we (Europeans) were crazy to let them (Asians) into Europe and that we would go the way of native Americans and be slaughtered by Arabs and Pakistanis. I pointed out to him that this was a distressingly racist view. Like all died in the wool racists he said that he wasn't racist and didn't mind Asians per-se... as long as they all stayed in Asia. I quickly ended the conversation.

Following this conversation it struck me how far we have come in Britain over the decades. Doubtless our country is riddled with seriously racist views. But even the racists know that their views don't make for acceptable conversation between passing strangers. Few people in Britain, however dodgy, would think it likely to be OK to come out with this Alf Garnet crap to a total stranger, particularly a long haired old hippy. Mind you, maybe the bloke was just eccentric. I did discover over the ensuing days that he was capable of getting angry and pissed off at almost anything. Yes... the ensuing days. By coincidence – (or was he following me?) - the German racist ended up in the same harbour as me on 10 separate nights in less than a fortnight. More often than not we'd be the only two cruising boats in and he'd treat me to more of his delightful views.

Kristiansund. What can I say. Not a lot. The only thing to recommend it was the traditional boat museum. An open air collection of buildings and various bits of stuff of the sea, plus a whole pile of beautiful old wooden boats on pontoons. All lovingly varnished and painted, they ranged from old lifeboats, through fishing boats, to a racing yacht from about 1920. Loads of old mannies, also looking like exhibits, sat around smoking ancient curly pipes and complaining in Norwegian that their wives wanted them at home mowing the lawn. I spoke to one chap about it. Though called a museum, the boats are mostly privately owned and maintained.

I did a bit of food shopping. Apropos of nothing at all, all the eggs in Norway are white. If you are old enough you will remember a time when most eggs in Britain were white and it was thought of as somehow special if you got a brown one. Ever on the lookout for a marketing opportunity, British chickens started laying only brown eggs to appeal to the punters. Now we scarcely ever see a white one. Norwegian chickens have either never hit upon this wheeze or it's gone full circle and now everyone wants white eggs.

The following day was a phew-what-a-scorcher and I motored with the main up a shortcut through skerries towards the wide, clean-sided, protected main channel, the Trondheimsleia. I was, of course, followed by the German. At one point the channel through the skerries got narrow and I slowed down from five knots to three to pick a careful way through. After I had successfully passed through the difficult bit, a dirty great hydrofoil ferry about 150 feet long and forty feet wide hurtled through the channel in the opposite direction. I looked at his signal on the AIS. He was doing thirty knots. At least he buzzed the German and gave him a fright as he was just coming up to the narrow bit.

The rest of the 58 mile trip was a motor in hot sun with only one mishap. My camera – a fairly old SLR inherited from my dad – decided to pack up. Something electrical I think. Stupidly, since Anna and I have acquired loads of cameras in various ways over the years, this was the only one I'd brought. There was no way I was going hundreds more miles through this stunning scenery without a camera.

I tied up for the night in yet another perfect harbour. The Island of Storfosna is about 2 miles across and nature has, of course, provided it with a big round hole in the middle with water 8 m deep and an entrance forty metres wide. Man has added to nature's work a pile of perfectly good pontoons, toilets and showers. Of course the German was there, and a nice Dutch steel yacht called Aap Kusanaq at anchor in the middle of the bay.

I cycled about looking for information about fast ferries to Norway's second largest city, Trondheim, which was 30 miles out of my way but would provide camera and camera repair shops, as well as internet access. This last I needed for a work thing, so that I could register an interest in enhanced early retirement and thence spend the majority of most years swanning about on boats.

Storfosna is an incredibly green farming island. This time at 63°40′ north, it had lush green fields, straight tall trees, big prosperous looking farmhouses, round hay bales in the fields, a shop, a pub and small industry. I repeat, it is 2 miles across and 63°40′ north.

I went into the transport-cafe style pub to ask about ferries and it was a bit like I imagine a trip to the American mid-west to be. Ten lumpen lads in various types of overalls – and the sort of American rounder caps that people wear backwards to make themselves look brain damaged - sat in rows at a single table, their mouths open and hamburgers held in mid air as I entered. Dolly Parton was on the jukebox. A big, burly woman with a died blonde '50s hairdo was cooking up chips and stuff behind a stainless steel counter. She explained that there was only a ferry here once every few days. I might have better luck at the next town on the mainland, Brekstad, but she didn't know. It wouldn't have surprised my if she had added *'because I've never been off the island'*.

Round about midnight, at 63 40′ north I was inside the boat club bog-block building trying to read a wee pamphlet. But the artificial lighting was poor, so I went outside so that I could see better.

So the next morning it was off motorsailing the ten miles or so to uninspiring town of Brekstad. Here, amongst the widely spaced

Bessaker

new wooden buildings, I found both free wi-fi access - courtesy of the old bloke running the Brekstad Hotel - and a camera shop. The latter was not free and I paid an exorbitant Norwegian price for a bottom of the range digital camera. Business concluded, I set off north again, having gone about sixteen miles out of my way.

If I've ever bought a camera before, I've then spent several winter days desperately searching for something worth photographing. Typically ending up with endless shots of half dead twigs in the garden and flat, grey, dull landscapes. Within half an hour of buying this camera, having only just got it out of the box and not yet read the destructions, I was passing through stunning mountain scenery, with twee villages crowded round the coast, lighthouses that looked like they'd been designed by Disney and huge skies with billowing clouds.

This was another long trip. sixty three miles. I motorsailed into the wind at first, but as I changed course to the east and the wind went more northerly I got some push from the sails and after six p.m. was beating towards our destination in a race with the much larger Dutch yacht Aap Kusanaq. A nice gentle sail at the end of a long sunny day. I'd decided to stop at a tiny hamlet right on the main route – Bessaker. You will not need me to tell you who else had decided to stop there. In fact there was quite an international community. Zoph, the German racist, the Dutch yacht anchored round the corner and a 26ft Danish yacht sailed by an ostensibly extraordinarily pissed Danish bloke. He lives in Bodø, up

above the Arctic Circle where I was
heading, so was sailing south to
Denmark and, ultimately he claimed, the
Caribbean. A long haul for a 26 footer,
but he'd already been to Spitzbergen
solo, so perhaps not. This was the first
cruising boat I'd seen that was actually
smaller than Zoph.

Bessaker

Bessaker is a wee village full of
tourist huts built right down to the
water's edge and at that time stuffed full
of fishing Germen. Each had an
aluminium speedboat with a chartplotter
and some serious looking fishing kit. I
tied up on the private pontoon next to
them. Nobody ever seems to move you
on from private pontoons and the like in
Norway. I think they probably remain
quietly outraged that you've had the audacity to tie up to their private space but
are too polite to mention it. Verdant pasture surrounded the village and high up
on the mountains above were a load of whirring wind turbines.

I had a wee chat with some of the Germanglers and they expressed surprise
at the size of Zoph and the Danish boat. During the conversation I mentioned to
the Dane that my boat was only 2.8m wide. The Germen fell about in
astonishment. *'You've come all the way from Scotland in a 2.8m boat!?'* It took some
time to calm them down and explain that Zoph was 2.8m wide, not 2.8m long. I
went to sleep that night in the light of the massive spotlight that glared out over
the silent and deserted fishing quay that was, anyway, perfectly light due to the
sun! Electricity must be free in Norway. They just burn it either for fun or
specifically to annoy me. Perhaps they are encouraged to burn it willy-nilly by
the sight of dozens of huge wind turbines busily turning atop the hills around
town.

Norway's future, it seems to me, unlike almost everywhere else in the world,
is assured forever, barring alien – or perhaps American - invasion. They will not
be phased by wee blips like 'credit crunches'. They have used and continue to
use vast quantities of oil money to build a massive civil engineering
infrastructure. This is Norway's Victorian period. All the really serious
engineering happened in Britain in the nineteenth century. In Norway it's
happening now.

Of course bridges, tunnels and harbours don't last literally forever, but with
a population of four and a half million, when the oil runs out they will easily
have enough hydro power to run Norway several times over. They have

millions of hectares of forest which can be grown sustainably. All the wind power is just an added bonus. Then, forever, they can export power and trees to the rest of us.

As the rest of the world fills up with people they will be clamouring for the wide open spaces and the beautiful countryside and coastline of Norway will end up hooching with rich touros scattering their money about. All they need for this to happen is a bit of currency revaluation and they can remain rich for the rest of time through tourism and energy industries. In the meantime, they are doing very nicely thank you and just biding their time. What a shame Scotland never had any oil. Perhaps we could have done the same.

The following day was another motorsail, this time a mere 46 miles to Rørvik. Of course I was shadowed by the German, who motors faster than Zoph, but I managed to beat him a couple of times by taking the inside short-cut through the rocks while he stuck to the main channel. Eventually he motored ahead however and I was joined in sailing by Aap Kusanaq.

What I took to be a pod of largish and sluggish dolphins following the boats the Dutch later swore were pilot whales. I accepted the identification as it gave me a new species I'd not seen before.

I continued to try sailing in the afternoon but after a while was headed by both tide and wind and ended up motoring into Rørvik just behind the Dutch steel yacht, which hung about tentatively in the harbour as I motored ahead, found a pontoon, tied up, then guided them into another, larger pontoon and took their lines for them. Well, there were only two of them on board and a whole one of me on Zoph.

Afterwards I had quite a long chat with the bloke of the couple. They'd commissioned the hull and built the rest themselves. Nice job too. It's an odd fact that the most seaworthy, tough, seagoing, capable, solid boats in Europe are built by a nation which sails about mostly on canals and shallow, tideless puddles in force twos. After I'd returned home in the autumn the crew of Aap Kusanaq emailed a couple of rather dull photos of Zoph, which was nice.

Rørvik was another rather uninspiring looking town I'm afraid. But perhaps we should take inspiration from the fact that this isolated rural town, population 2,700, has shipbuilding, oil industry, several ferries a day, a factory making fibreglass motorboats by the thousand, loads of shops, suburbs, indeed everything (and more) that you might expect from a town a hundred times its size in Scotland. I wonder if the Norwegian counting system is different and they miss a

The Rorvik Museum, being Norway's worst designed building, is of course award-winning

nought off the end of population figures. By all accounts the town's population is 2700, but perhaps it's really 27,000... or 270,000.

Torghatten. Spot the hole in the rock

I was reminded of the time I first visited Norway – as a penniless student hitching around southern Scandinavia in 1982. I got a lift from a slightly pissed bloke who, on

dropping me off, assured me it was only three miles to the next village. I collapsed exhausted into my tent by the roadside a few hours later without having found the village. Later someone explained that a Norwegian mile was... ten miles.

Rørvik also has an ultra-modern new museum, which was apparently nominated for the Mies van der Rohe architecture prize. I'm surprised it didn't win, since it was a wholly misconceived, out of place and badly designed structure. Designed, as all High Architecture is, only for the immediate visual impact, it had windows none of which anyone over four feet tall could see out of, looked abysmal from the sea side, which is where most people arriving in Rørvik (by ferry), will see it from, made bad use of exclusively imported materials and, at two years old, was falling apart already. In two words, brilliant architecture.

The next day, as chance would have it, I again did exactly 46 miles. As I motored north through the narrow channel north of Rørvik a big catamaran motored directly towards us on a collision course from the north. I did the proper thing and immediately turned twenty degrees to starboard as we were on a reciprocal course, muttering under my breath about the inability of the Norges to follow the collision regulations and confidently expecting him not to change course. To my surprise he also turned immediately twenty degrees to starboard. As we passed port to port I saw the red ensign and the name on the stern, under which was written 'Southampton'. This was the first British boat I'd seen on the move in Norway and practically the only boat overtly to display a knowledge of the coll. regs. Are we a particularly anal country do you suppose?

I motorsailed at first in heavy cloud then showers mixed with a bit of sun. As I passed round the island of Dolma I saw that the German was again chasing me and by the other end of the island the Dutch boat hove into view on the port

Canine Canoeing

side, having left earlier and come the long way round by the scenic route. By Leka Island we had all switched places as the German passed me and I passed the Dutch.

Near the end of the trip was Torghatten, a bizarre mountain with a hole, apparently natural, right through it. Through this hole you can clearly see the sky if you are a couple of miles away to the south west. I duly put a waypoint on the chartplotter for the best viewpoint. A huge ferry went past. The AIS said it had the same destination as me, Bronnoysund, yet it turned left before it should have. Worried, I checked the charts for low bridges or shallows en route, but my intended track seemed fine. I looked again at the AIS. The ferry had stopped exactly on my waypoint. A huge cruise liner went past. It did the same. In all three ships turned off the track, went to my waypoint to look through a hole in the mountain, then turned round and went to Brønnøysund. I duly headed up a wee shortcut through the skerries to have a look myself. A quite odd phenomenon but in the end just a hole in a mountain.

Personally I think the Norwegians drilled the hole themselves to attract tourists. Given the amount of rock they must need to built all those harbours, sticking a hole in a mountain would be a piece of piss.

Having gone off the direct course to Bronnoysund gave me a better heading and as the gentle breeze had increased a bit I sailed most of the rest of the way to the large, new, substantial visitors' pontoon in the small town of Bronnoysund. Of course the German was there already, expressing massive confusion at the eccentric behaviour of all the ferries and cruise ships around here.

A Swedish neighbour in Bronnoysund

The Hurtigrute in the distance

Some time after midnight I heard an engine and looked out to the stern. No more than a foot away were the davits, dinghy and self-steering gear of an old, seventy foot wooden Swedish ketch. I went ashore to help its single occupant with his lines, but he didn't need any help. He said he usually sailed alone and though he had another crew today, as it happened, he hadn't bothered getting him on deck to manoeuvre this monster into a space between two boats only about three feet longer than it.

Only half way up Norway

Having had difficulty getting my credit or debit cards to work in the automated fuel stations as I moved further north, I was relieved the next morning to find at the pumps a defunct credit card paying machine and a human being taking cash for diesel. Ah the old ways are the best.

Another longish 51 mile trip the next day to Nesna, teetering just off the brink of the Arctic Circle, but this was an easy, gentle motor in flat calm up an easy and obvious sheltered inner lane past a thousand small islands and a few big ones. I saw two white tailed sea eagles on that passage. The first was near the island of Vega, which apparently is a world heritage site, but nobody can tell me why. The second bird probably wasn't a white tailed sea eagle, now I think about it. I saw it flying near the island of Tomma, so it was probably a Tommahawk.

I'd been monitoring the decreasing length of the night as I headed north using the sunrise and sunset information on the GPS. During this trip, according to my GPS, sunrise became earlier than sunset. Is this possible? We weren't at the Arctic Circle yet. But if the day is not in fact exactly evenly distributed around midnight, then is it possible that sunrise on June 17th is earlier than sunset at the end of the previous day? I made my brain hurt a bit thinking about this. On a nice evening I went under full sail towards Nesna, but still needed a wee push from the motor to make decent time. The visitors' pontoon, in about 1.3m of water, was right inshore and practically in the clubhouse. God knows how bigger boats find their way in there.

Windmills and shipping bearing down on us.

The boat harbour in Nesna had free showers, a living room with big settees and a telly and a computer with free internet access. The Harbourmaster (a rather grand term for the retired bloke who takes turns with his mates to pester you for money on arrival), invited me on his boat - which was hauled out to be antifouled - for a drink. We spoke about boating and fishing in this part of the world. Apparently most of the boats stay in the water all year, since the best fishing is in winter. At 66° north they all go out fishing for cod in bleeding February, if you can believe that.

Unlike in Britain, the huddled masses of Norway don't seem to head en-masse for the more grotesque Mediterranean resorts in the summer. So places like Nesna, nearly at the Arctic Circle, look like old-fashioned British seaside resorts, with caravan parks, amusements, flumes etc. The town was reasonably buzzing with German camper-trucks and folk down from Arctic Mo Irana for a bit of mass seaside tourism.

I didn't visit the relatively major inland town of Mo Irana. This is something of a blessing, since I find it impossible to say without adopting the tones of Vic Reeves on Shooting Stars intoning *'Iranoo'*.

There was a Dutch folkboat of around 24 feet in Nesna which was even smaller than the Danish one and holds the record for the smallest foreign boat I saw in Norway. The other distinguishing feature of Nesna was that the German yacht wasn't there!

Having lived in Aberdeen for years, I can't help thinking that Nesna ought to be spelled N.E.S.N.A. and stand for 'North East Scotland Navigation Authority' or something.

From Nesna, or N.E.S.N.A. the Arctic Circle was just over the horizon.

Arcticulating

The next day was to be Arctic Circle day, when I reached the waypoint I'd had in the GPS since south of Bergen. As far as I can gather the Arctic Circle, which apparently moves about a bit, is currently at 66°33'39", which is where my waypoint was.

I motored north in a flat calm. There is a big monument, supposedly at the Arctic Circle and consisting of a globe and some rings, on the island of Vikingen. What a load of nonsense. It's placed at 66°32'. Presumably it was just a convenient and prominent place, but it's clearly the wrong place.

This reminded me, a pedant with a hand-held GPS, of a visit to a monument marking the Tropic of Capricorn in Australia. I pointed out to its guardians that their monument to the tropic was miles out of place. With typical Australian 'she'll-be-right' and lack of respect for actual facts they said "Oh yeah, we moved it when we moved the shop". "You can't just go moving major theoretical phenomena about!" I protested. 'Where's the North Pole gone Mother'. 'Oh I put it over there, it was getting in the way'.

The wind increased and I managed full sail for a couple of miles to the <u>real</u> Arctic Circle, as marked by my waypoint, where I gave a ceremonial verbal fanfare. Rounding a headland I turned more directly into the wind.

Passing a small sheltered anchorage mentioned in the pilot I saw a strangely non-Norwegian looking sailing boat in it. Why didn't it look Norwegian? For one thing it was swinging at anchor, which few Norgians ever do. It was also sort of... well British looking. As I approached it appeared to be flying a red ensign. Since Norgian and British flags have about the same colours I'm usually wrong about this, but in this case I was right. I motored around it. There appeared to be no-one aboard, but as I circled, a small figure on a hill ashore started gesticulating. Eventually I saw it was a woman who was shouting 'My skipper's on board'. From this I assumed it was some sort of sail training boat. But a bloke then appeared from the cabin and it became obvious that this was the woman's husband, who she apparently calls 'my skipper' to complete strangers.

The boat was called 'Vagrant of Clyde' and was, I was told after I'd mis-identified it as a Rustler, a Bowman 40. I always expect boats called something 'of Clyde' to be full of

Leaving Nesna

Glaswegians. Of course they are usually manned by posh English folk who keep their boats in places like Kip marina and Vagrant of Clyde proved to be no exception.

For no good reason it struck me at the time that that there are only two sorts of Wegians in the world – Nor and Glas. Three years later, as Zoph was circumnavigating Ireland, we visited Galway and I discovered a third sort of Wegian, the Gal. Why these three disparate places should be the only ones to adopt this suffix for its denizens I do not know.

Vagrant of Clyde was heading north as her crew liked the high latitudes. Liked them so much, in fact that they'd covered 55,000 miles in sailing round the world, via Iceland, Greenland, the North Cape, Chile, New Zealand, the Beagle Channel, the Falklands, South Georgia and Antarctica. The chap managed to point all this out to me in the first minute's conversation, by the way. They were extraordinarily posh but very jolly and friendly.

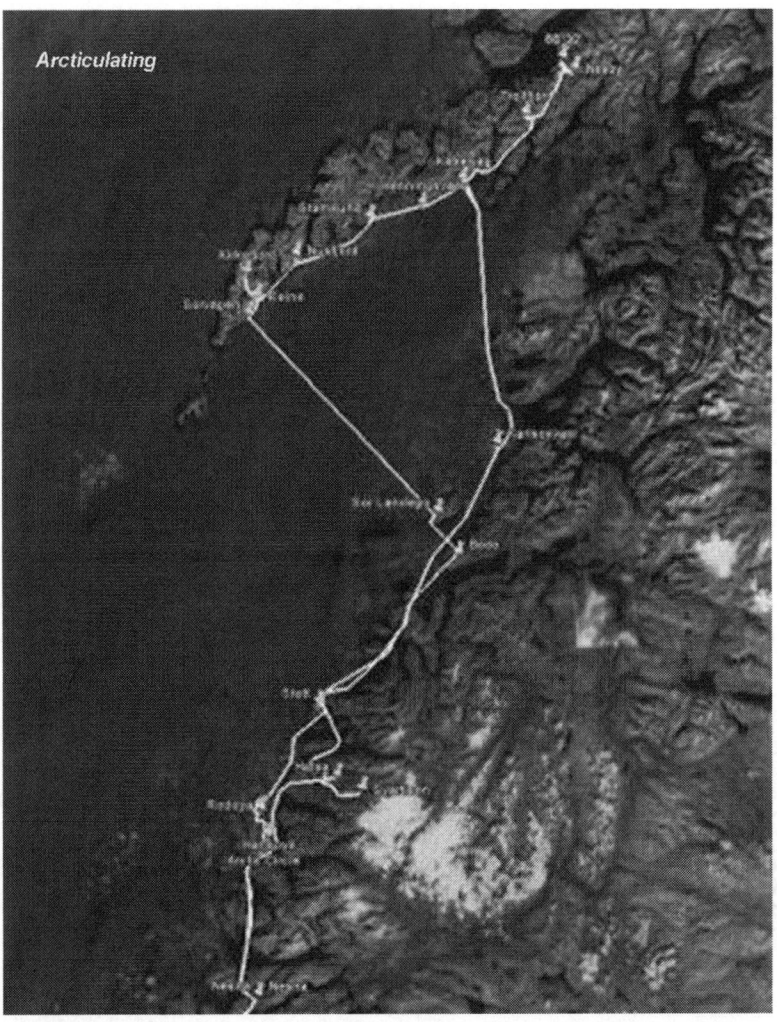

Arcticulating

I had intended to carry on another 25 miles or so to Støtt, but after I left the anchorage it began to get considerably windier. Only fifteen to eighteen knots true, but right on the nose and a bit splashy. I'd also reached a significant goal – the Arctic Circle - so I thought, 'why push it' and looked in the pilot book for somewhere to stop. After all, the Vagrants had decided to stay put because of the conditions and they were used to the Southern Ocean, so why shouldn't I have a half day for a change?

A mile away to the right was a perfect anchorage, to the left a few options but the easiest was a good set of pontoons outside a restaurant, with water and electricity, perfectly sheltered from the north. These were about a mile and a half away and twenty minutes or so after changing my plans Zoph was safely tied up and I had the kettle on while it blew 25 knots outside.

That's why you don't, by and large, need to do any real passage planning in Norway. Indeed most Norwegian sailors don't know what you are talking about if you mention passage planning. They just head off whenever they want without considering the tides and if conditions deteriorate look in a book and choose from a range of harbours something perfect and not more than a couple of miles away. There's nearly always somewhere to go, whatever happens. My perfect pontoons were at Selvag, on the Island of Rødøya, whose entire road system I Brompted about that evening.

The following morning I motored north up a narrow channel from Rødøya and raised the main when I came out into the open to join Vagrant of Clyde and a Harmony 38, which was sailing in from a side channel. Pretty soon both cutters, Zoph and Vagrant, were under full sail, with the motor going off at one pm. I was pleased to see that Zoph sailed as close to the wind as the Bowman. Or to put it another way, the Bowman is just as crap to windward as Zoph, though she did go a little bit faster and caught us up slowly. The proper sailing only lasted an hour or so. Soon it was back to engine plus full sail, then engine only as the wind went on the nose for the rest of the 54 mile trip to Bodø.

Bodø is a surprisingly big and lively town, with folk sitting out in the cafes, a

Vagrant of Clyde

The mountains south of Bodo

huge marina full of local boats and some foreigners staying long term, as well as twenty or so visiting yachts, of which Zoph, of course, was the smallest.

On a pontoon as I entered the harbour I found Tarka of Lorne, the forty foot Hallberg Rassy, last seen in the marina in Kirkwall claiming to be heading to the Lofoten Islands. Here she was locked up with the owners perhaps gone home.

I rafted up on a 40ft Swedish yacht. Right behind Zoph on the quay was another Hallberg Rassy, a beautiful new Hallberg Rassy 62. I went for a wander. Of course the German was there, but so was Vagrant and I was asked on board for a coffee. An odd thing to offer after 9 pm I thought.

The coffee turned eventually into a single beer but we had a good long chat, mostly horror stories about their cruising. This included the coast of Chile, where apparently if you aren't prepared to set sail in forty knots of wind you never go anywhere. Their scariest trip was directly from the Falklands to the UK, during which they met a storm that knocked them over and broke nearly everything. It didn't seem to affect their attitude to cruising adversely, however. He used apparently to be Military Attaché to the British Embassy in Venezuela, whatever that is, and frightfully posh. I did wonder if it was a bit odd for a military attaché to a British embassy to want to call his boat 'Homeless Glaswegian'.

I reckoned that real midnight here at 14°22' east, with the clock set at 2 hours after GMT on June the twentieth, was 01:03 and 28.8 seconds, to be reasonably exact. The sun was on Zoph at that time and at 01:34 it came in through a port side window and lit up the GPS, showing the time and the lat/long position. Proper proof of genuine midnight sun.

The next morning the Swedes I was rafted onto, who had considerable problems communicating to each other what to do with ropes and the like, wanted to leave. I untied Zoph and motored in a circle to tie to the Quay ahead of the big Hallberg vacated by the Swedes. An old gent got off the big Hallberg Rassy and helped with my bow line.

...and yet more Bodoceous mountains

I did some shopping in Bodø, for
Lofoten charts, which I was short of,
having only bought about 200 charts
for the trip thus far. The German was
of course also buying charts in the
same shop. Though my primary
means of navigation was the laptop
chartplotter, only an insane person
would stake their life on a Windows
PC not crashing at a crucial moment.

Therefore I also needed full paper chart coverage of the whole route.

You could successfully navigate the east coast of Britain with an Imray
1:200,000 chart and a pilot book. Norway is so astonishingly strewn with rocks
and islands creating a mass of intricate channels that you really need the
maximum scale, 1:50,000 charts. The Norwegian versions of these charts are
mostly excellent, simply numbered sequentially all along the coast from Oslo
and cost twenty quid a pop.

The Admiralty produce many of the equivalent charts, outdated versions of
which are available online for about £2.70 each, some of which are as good as the
Norwegian versions and many of which are entirely crap. Over the winter I
would eagerly unwrap a whole series of charts brought by the postie. I would
find one filled with detail of every rock and channel. The next chart would
overlap with it and would have the same area of sea just coloured pale blue for
mile after mile with absolutely no detail and the legend 'dangerous shoals'
written right across it. The Admiralty's 'dangerous shoals' are, needless to say,
the Norwegians' main small boat channels.

Despite the paucity of information on many charts they would have served
in an emergency to navigate to the nearest big town, so day after day I
religiously stowed away the previous day's charts and sought out the next day's
using my actually quite meticulous and rather anal cataloguing system. From
autumn to spring the same large
scale chart of part of the Forth
stays on my chart table all the
time and if I ever disappeared off
the edge of it – say by sailing
eight miles and past the island of
Inchkeith – I'd think I'd had a real
adventure. In the summer I
discard at least two 1:50,000
charts every day and unwrap
another two for the next day's
passage. If I'd have paid full price

Sør Landego with Zoph and the German Racist

for these charts it'd be far and away the most expensive part of cruising.

That day in Bodø I also bought a mains electric cooker. This may seem a little eccentric, but I had already emptied one bottle of gas and was aware that once all three were used I had a problem. There's no bottled butane sold in Norway, only propane. Therefore, whenever connected to shore power I could cook on a couple of rings sitting on top of the gas stove.

Having failed to find out how to have a shower in the expensive and facility-free harbour in Bodø I left. It wasn't a day to make a long trip, with quite strong northerlies forecast and a lot of rain, so I sailed on a broad reach in eight to fifteen knots of apparent wind the short nine mile passage to Landegode Island where, at Sor-Landego, there is another little village with a population of about four, an impossibly sheltered natural harbour and a shop. It's a fairly obscure place so Zoph was the only boat tied to the long guest pontoon.

Bodo at midnight

...and here's the proof

I went for a walk around the pleasant, lush farmland and hills, primarily to get phone reception. In three months in Norway Sor-Landego was the only place I came across where I couldn't get mobile phone reception in the harbour. I had to walk a few hundred yards. This is in stark contrast to the rural west Scotland, in which there's only one place every fifty miles or so where you can get reception, if you happen to have your phone on the right network..

When I returned, the bloody German racist was tied up the other side of the pontoon. What were the chances? I thought he was supposed to be in a hurry. He had also had a lazy half day, in preparation for the assault on Lofoten tomorrow.

I tried my swanky new onboard showering arrangement for the first time in anger that evening. This posh and devilishly clever device consists basically of a pump action weedkiller spray from B&Q. The bagpipe type where you pump it up beforehand and then get a continuous spray. The plumbing system consists of a kettle of boiling water and 1.5 kettles of cold water poured in at the start. How sophisticated can you get? It was, perhaps surprisingly, reasonably effective, though it did feel a little like standing outside in a fine drizzle.

Floated to Lofoten

Sailing the 42 miles across the Vestfjord to Lofoten was probably the best sail of the trip so far. I was woken up by the German's bow thruster as he left. I got up quickly and followed him out. Full sail went up just outside the harbour and I had a beam reach in full sun and a force four, with the line of the Lofoten mountains clearly visible nearly fifty miles away.

Can anyone ever really have believed that the earth was flat? We are persuaded that the ancients thought it was. But surely they didn't all live a long way from the sea or somewhere it was always foggy. On any decent clear day you can plainly see that bits of boats are hidden below the horizon, while their masts stick up above it. Surely all those ancient Greeks, swanning around the Mediterranean could quite clearly have spotted that ships came up over the horizon and didn't just resolve themselves out of the mist.

...as I approached Lofoten the cloud cleared

Approaching Lofoten

On this day, sailing to Lofoten, the peaks which just peeked over the horizon began to resolve themselves into mountains as we sailed around the revolving earth towards them.

The German seemed to be heading off in erratic directions and at one point tried his spinnaker, which pushed him off down wind. Around the middle of the Vestfjord I entered a line of low cloud and could no longer see the mountains, whilst the wind headed us a bit and became a bit fluky. I still managed over four knots in the right direction though.

A dramatic change occurred when about ten miles from our destination. I left the low cloud, the sun came out and the spiky peaks of the 'Lofoten Wall' rose ahead of us, speckled with snow and with billows of fluffy white cloud leaking out through the valleys. At the same time the wind backed and increased to around twenty knots true, gusting 25. Zoph shot along at up to seven knots and sailed right into Sørvågen harbour, on Moskensøya Island, five minutes behind the German, who had left in his 45ft boat while I was still abed. It's not often Zoph gets the nice reaches she likes best and wins the race.

Midnight in the Arctic

Near A

Just a few miles away, off the end of Moskensøya, is reputed to be Norway's worst bit of water, the Moskenstraum Maelstrom. From it we have taken the very word 'maelstrom'. Edgar Allen Poe wrote of it thus: "In five minutes the sea was lashed into an ungovernable fury... Here the vast bed of the waters seamed and scarred into a thousand conflicting channels, burst suddenly into frenzied convulsion – heaving, boiling, hissing". These reassuring words are reproduced in the pilot book. I really wish I hadn't read them before making the crossing

There was one small space available on the guest pontoon in Sørvågen and as I tied up next to a 48 ft gin palace I reflected that I had, in fact, floated low to Lofoten. It was June 21st – midsummer's night – and I had travelled 1311.5 miles from Port Edgar in thirty one days sailing since May 6th. Over 41 miles a day including the days pootling slowly around Bergen and going practically nowhere. It hadn't been difficult but it had been a long way solo and I felt a certain elation at having reached my goal, not least because I could now call the log 'Floating low to Lofoten'.

Actually, I realised that now I was not floating so low to Lofoten. Indeed the antifouling was appearing worryingly above the water and the cockpit was alarmingly empty of water, even when motoring at speed. Probably I should have marked where the waterline was before and after filling the boat with booze. I could then have divided the difference to create a scale – say in fifty litre sections – and would have had an accurate measure of how much beer was left. I should also, definitely, not have listened to Anna when she told me I had plenty of beer and surely 450 cans and 250 bottles was enough. I was only just over three weeks into my Norgian odyssey, with a good two months to go and already the ballast was running low.

The sapping of the supplies was assuaged slightly because I was invited aboard the new Princess 48 gin palace next door for a beer, by the Norwegian owner and his two Canadian chums. A boat you have to take your shoes off before boarding is not really a boat. It was nice of them but the experience was a bit odd. Having taken the trouble to invite me, they just stared blankly into space at everything I said and seemed relieved when I left soon after. Either I said something to upset them or my patented boat shower was not doing its job and I was stinking the place out and polluting the white leather sofas.

Sørvågen is right next to the famously twee and ludicrously peremptorily named village of Å, which has been done up as a tourist attraction. I Brompted there and it certainly was attracting the touros, by the coach and campervan load. The wee houses and sheds on stilts over the water were almost painfully cute. This could not be said of the racks and racks of dead cod hanging out to dry practically as far as the eye could see. This was to be a constant, whiffy theme in Lofoten.

The next day I got the sails up in the tiny narrow harbour and had a gentle run out, but the wind was fickle and soon died so it was on with the motor for the few miles to the village of Reine. This is a whaling station and apparently headquarters of the main pro whaling campaign group, if you can imagine such a thing. It's also the picture on the front of the pilot book and on a thousand adverts for Norwegian tourism. Its startling backdrop of curvaceous mountains makes it a real chocolate box favourite.

But I left without going ashore and motored through the eighteen metre high bridge into the Kirkefjord. I did think of trying the nearer twelve metre high bridge at lowish tide, since Zoph's air draught is about twelve metres, but decided on the cautious route. At the head of the Kirkefjord, in hot sun, I tied to the pier used by tourist boats and headed up a path leading up to a high saddle of land and over to the wild north side of the Lofotens, where all the best beaches are. Looking down the valley to the beach below was stunning. I didn't want to have to climb the 500 ft path twice however, so went back down to Zoph and motored in a flat calm and hot sun to Reine for the night. I got the last wee sheltered space in the shallow harbour on a bit of pontoon about 20 ft long with a tiny, shallow, rock-strewn turning space. Just big enough for wee Zoph to moor with her bow sticking out over the end.

Reine proved to be a valuable lesson on the virtues of travelling in a small boat. There were about ten foreign yachts in the harbour and apart from a German one of about 32 ft - tiny for Norway - they were all at least 40 ft long. The 40 ft Nordship managed to look small beside the racist German's boat, which in turn looked tiny compared to an american 55 ft Hallberg Rassy and the 62 ft Hallberg I'd seen in Bodø, which was also in the harbour.

Ah

Aaaaaaaa!

Several of the crews were complaining that they'd have liked to go up the Kirkefjord too, but their masts were all too tall for the eighteen metre bridge. The next morning a large German yacht tried to leave but kept hitting the rocks as it was low tide, so had to wait several hours. Zoph just left without incident. A couple of days later the skipper of the Nordship, which had to take an outer pontoon, exposed to the west, confessed that they'd had a rotten night. With strong winds blowing her on and popping out the fenders they'd had to set an anchor watch to shove the fenders back periodically.

Everyone who wants to cruise any sort of distance seems to think that the minimum size of boat you need is around forty feet these days. Unless you have a family of eight this is nonsense. A good, well found, seaworthy 27 footer is as good as anything. You can handle it yourself without needing to rely on a crew. It's actually easier in bad weather, since all the sails – and hence the forces – are smaller. You can find moorings more easily. In the Baltic and the Netherlands, where they moor between piles, none of the modern boats will fit in the spaces. They all raft up outside while Zoph takes one of the empty spaces between the piles. In Scandinavia, where everyone rafts up, nobody minds Zoph rafting on them because she's small and because big boats are unlikely to raft up outside Zoph. Your raftee limits the size of the raft and a small boat is like a full stop. Zoph was almost always the furthest out in any raft.

Don't go in a 27ft dinghy, but a proper heavyweight like Zoph is, I reckon, about the optimum cruising boat. She is also smaller than nearly everything in

Norway. Oh yes, I almost forgot, a 27 ft yacht is also likely to be a lot cheaper than a 50 ft one, both to buy and keep in marinas.

Reine lived up to its fantastic aesthetic reputation as I Brompted about in it and – glory of glories – I fulfilled a two year quest and actually managed to buy a bag of ice in a Norwegian shop! After being looked on as clinically insane even for asking in the rest of Scandinavia, the Lofots actually buy and sell ice. The village of Reine isn't particularly lovely, but its setting, surrounded by perfect sweeping peaks and 'U' valleys that look like copper-plate handwriting on which the sun never sets in summer, is startling.

It didn't rain in Reine, but it chucked it down in Nusfjord, my next stop, some 12 miles away. There was a surprising amount of chop given the forecast light breeze, but it was on the nose a bit and increasing. Zoph was the focus of tourist attention as we entered Nusfjord's preserved old harbour and tied up, the only boat on the guest pontoon. Like Å it's just for the touros now and the whole village is in fact a museum – or a series of museums really – including (I kid you not) a museum of cod liver oil.

I sauntered about a bit in the pissing down rain and brushed up a bit on my Lofot culture and history, with the help pf a film shown by a gay Swedish bloke who ran the café and, though employed as an expert guide, knew not one solitary thing about the Lofotens on account of having arrived from Stockholm two days before to do the job for a couple of months.

Lovely

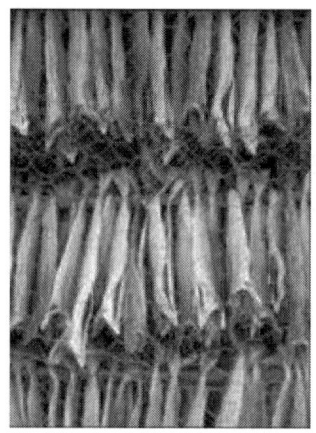

The Lofoten economy has, apparently, since Viking times at least, been fundamentally about cod. Bizarrely they fish it out of the water in a 3 month fishing season, split the fish open, hang them outside to dry on huge wooden racks some hundred metres long, then sell the actual fish to southern European countries.

The importance of the stuff in the southern diet is underlined by the names for Lofoten dried cod in different languages. It's bacalhau in Portuguese, bacalao in Spanish, bakaịlao in Basque, bacallà in Catalan, bakalar in Croatian and baccalà in Italian. The heads are exported to west African countries where they

Kirkefjord

are bunged in stews. You'd have thought this a shaky basis for an entire economy, but they've been doing it for centuries and it seems to work.

You may be thinking: "Well that doesn't sound too bad. 3 months fishing in the land of the midnight sun. June, July and August would be all right". But no. The fishing season is from February to April. The inconsiderate bloody fish insist on coming down to Lofoten then, to the apparently 'warmer waters' to spawn. It doesn't get light at all in February and for centuries folk have been going out into the arctic winter night in small rowing boats to catch fish to dry and send to Spain. I'm not sure I'd fancy it now, with huge fishing ships fitted with all mod cons, but in open rowing boats lit by candles? No ta.

Though the Norges don't appear to eat the filthy stuff themselves, this dried fish is deeply ingrained in Lofot culture. Quite often you'll see one or two fish heads stapled up over someone's door, apparently as decoration. It seems your average Lofot considers the desiccated gaping maw of a dead cod to be the height of aesthetic good taste. I'm afraid I can't share that view.

Zoph was still the only boat on the pontoon the next day and despite a wet and cold forecast I eventually decided to leave. Partly through the feeling that everyone else must be off having fun somewhere else. Whilst I'm not seeking vacationing crowds, I want somebody else about, sort of to validate my choice of

A cruising boat from the Czech Republic smaller than Zoph

holiday spot. Of course as soon as I'd decided to leave and was untying the lines the place was heaving with other boats. First the Nordship from Reine with a Norge skipper and a couple of Americans arrived. On the way out a Harmony 38 was coming in – the same one I'd seen on the long passage to Bødo, I think - and once out at sea another cruiser appeared and sailed in.

Reine

Reine

Also, just before I left, I spotted cruising boats smaller than Zoph. Six Czech canoeists hove into view. Five of them were just having a wee paddle the length and breadth of the Lofotens for a week or two. The sixth – a personable sort of young chap with a frightening handshake and a lot of apparently designer stubble – was paddling from Stavanger to the North Cape. That's around 1500 miles and up above 71° north, making my puny efforts in Zoph, with a kitchen, a bog, heating and an engine, look very wimpy. Mind you, his canoe was only just shorter than Zoph, at 6.5 metres.

It was a gusty day and under jib alone I was sometimes doing two knots and sometimes over six in too much wind. I'm not sure exactly how much wind there was since the bloody anemometer had packed up again, after working OK for nearly a month. I told myself that I must chuck it out and invest in a decent one.

On the way to Stamsund I passed just inshore of what I took to be a lobbo pot buoy. Just too late I realised that it actually supported a net strung out from the shore floating just below the surface on a line of small cork floats. Zoph went right over the line. If she were a more modern boat, with a short fin and a skeg or a separate rudder, we'd probably still be there. Even if it hadn't fouled the prop the line would have been caught between keel and rudder. Zoph's long keel with the rudder fixed directly to it just ran straight over it and out the other side.

...and again

I looked into Stamsund harbour where the pilot book told me to go, but there didn't seem anywhere to tie up so I tried the north harbour, which it also suggested. This was a bit run down and though we got a pontoon it was a bit crap and dishevelled. I Brompted into the rather dull town and there, not at all where the pilot book said, was a huge posh new concrete guest pontoon. I went back and moved the boat onto it.

Pretty soon the Nordship from Reine and Nusfjord appeared and its inept American crew members spied my Brompton. "Wow, what a great idea, a bicycle on a boat!" they waxed. "In Florida you see lots of yachts with cars and helicopters on board, but who would ever have thought of a bicycle!" Now I know Americans are stupid, firmly wedded to internal combustion engines and some of them are very rich, but surely even they would see a bicycle on a boat as a more practical option than a bleedin' helicopter. These two numpties were fooling no-one. They were pretending that everyone in their backward, practically third world country was a multi-billionaire. In reality they could only afford to sail in Norway by bumming a lift on their chum's boat.

There was some electricity left on one of the power points, so when I paid for the berth in the nearby hotel I asked the girl if I could buy a leccy card and then sell it back if I didn't use it. She questioned my integrity and suggested that I might use the card and then try to sell it back. I was bleedin' outraged. Apart from the fact that when used the cards are stamped with an indented marks to void them, this seemed most un-Norwegian to me. I asked her how many KWH were on the cards. She seemed to thing this an odd question "How should I know?" she said. "Well, because you are selling a commodity, you must know how much of it you are selling, surely. Is it one kilowatt-hour or a thousand?". She shrugged her shoulders, confused by the complexity of my argument. I went, somewhat churlishly, without leccy.

The next morning I left Stamsund under full sail and in high dudgeon for Henningsvær. This would be something of a milestone for me, as we'd put in here briefly two years before with Gordon Equinox and this year I'd had it as my Lofoten waypoint in the GPS since Bergen. When I told a friend I was off cruising Norway she sent me a photo of Henningsvær - another chocolate box staple - as a demonstration of how gorgeous it could be. I was able to send her,

A lovely Lofoten decoration in Nusfjord

by return, my own photo, taken from Equinox in more or less the same position on a beautiful sunny day.

After a fluky start the wind increased to perhaps twenty knots true and we sailed on a beam reach at between four and 6.5 knots on a dreich and showery day. Entering the harbour I was greeted from afar by a couple of excitable and pissed Glaswegian voices – lads working in a local shipyard I think. They waved pint glasses about and cheered my StAn's flag. I think they were a bit disappointed to hear my middle class English tones answer them.

A window in Henningsvær with a very Caledonian theme

I tied up on the pontoon used by Equinox two years before and had a squint at the gorgeous view. Which wasn't. With drizzle and cloud over the majestic spiky peaks I'm afraid Henningsvær looked rather less like aesthetic perfection.

A reasonably sober couple turned up in a motor boat and tied up the other side of the pontoon, while I helped a crowd of pissed partyers tie up their two wee gin palaces ahead of Zoph. I chatted to the bloke on the motorboat next door. He was down from Tromsø for a taste of the subtropical Lofotens for his summer holiday and heading further south. Stuck to the notice board detailing the exorbitant charges (£15 without the use of a shower or other significant facilities), was an envelope containing money and the words *"Thank you – Tarka of Lorne"* and dated the day before. What a remarkably honest, if elusive, bunch they must be. I seemed destined not to catch up with the Tarka crew as I had suggested in Kirkwall I might.

I never did catch up with Tarka in Norway, but the following year We were at Ardfern, south of Oban, on the way to the outer Hebrides. Tarka was there and I left a note aboard mentioning that I'd seen her several times in 2008. Eventually I got this email back from her skipper:

"I remember meeting you in Kirkwall. We left there on 23 June and went straight to Bødo unfortunately mainly in north/northeasterly winds; I think we did nearly 1000nm through the water! As you say we then left Tarka there for a few weeks and I went out with the family later and went to Lofoten arriving there on 21 June. We must have only just missed you as we were in Reine, Nusford ,Gulvika and arrived at Henningsvaar on 24 June. We then had to go back to Bødo for some of the crew to fly to Paris and I and my wife then had a leisurely sail down the coast to Trondheim arriving on 9 July. We spent a few days there and then flew home leaving Tarka at the pontoons. A few weeks later I returned with much the same crew as on the way out and we sailed Tarka back to Ardfern non-stop - this time going north of Muckle Flugga and down the west coasts of Shetland, Orkney and Scotland."

It had stopped raining the following day, on June

Henningsvaer snapped two years earlier on Equinox

26th, when Zoph left Henningsvær, though it was still overcast and dull as I motored, with a bit of help from the jib, to the old Lofoten ex-capital of Kabelvåg for a quick squint into the harbour, then on to the present Lofoten capital Svolvær, where Vagrant of Clyde was on the pontoon with a few other cruising boats. After a quick chat I headed on

Hurtigrute ship in Trollfjord

northwards through the fourteen metre bridge, chuckling smugly that it was too low for Vagrant, which was following me but had to take the long way round.

I wasn't chuckling a few minutes later as I was nearly killed by a speedboat coming through the bridge the other way at about 25 knots. We were on a head on collision course, so I turned twenty degrees to starboard. He duly turned to port. I turned a further thirty degrees to starboard. He turned to port to keep us on a collision course. In the end I was motoring hard out of the channel at ninety degrees to my previous course as he continued to change course to collide with me. With about three seconds to go before our mutually assured destruction he had a change of heart and put in a quick swerve to starboard, averting disaster. Folk walking over the bridge were surprised at the ferocity of tone and Anglo Saxon nature of the language with which I was expressing my feelings towards the retreating speedboat. I am told that Norgians have to pass some sort of test to drive a boat about. It is clear that this test does not include any mention of the collision regs.

I motored on to the startling Trollfjord, which we also visited aboard Equinox. This is only a mile and a half long, but very deep and narrow, with sheer cliff sides that for most of its length you can touch from the boat. I'd only just gone in when I was followed in by a huge Hurtigrute ferry, the sides of the

fjord dwarfing this large ship as it turned slowly in the narrow space, almost touching the walls. Quite surreal. The Harmony 38 also turned up in the Trollfjord, which is very much on the cruiser route.

Then it was on northwards again up the Raftsund, fast flowing in places and the strongest tide I'd experienced in

Trollfjord

Norway at four knots. Happily it
was with me. I crossed the fifteen
degrees east line of longitude and
was a full hour east of Greenwich,
one hour twelve minutes east of
Port Edgar.

Trollfjord

I checked out an anchorage in
the Raftsund then headed to the
north end where I made a pig's
ear of mooring fore and aft with a
stern anchor in the bay of Hanøy.
In leaping off the bow with a line I
very nearly lost the boat and had a
fleeting vision of me stuck on the
remote shore staring out at Zoph,
anchored in eight metres in the
middle of the freezing cold bay by
her stern. While I was calculating
how much the tide would fall and
deciding that she wouldn't hit the bottom a car stopped and its occupants stared
at me in dumbfounded disbelief. I decided against staying there. A few days
later a Bodø local casually mentioned that at this latitude nobody has stern
anchors because the tide is too big. I joined him in laughing at the soft southern
idea that you might actually moor fore and aft to a rock in this part of the world.
Naturally I didn't mention my own attempts.

I finally anchored in the pleasant pool at Nesøy, joining Vagrant, I'm afraid,
the crew of which might begin to think I was following them around. It took
three goes to get the anchor to dig in and even then I'm not sure how well it
would have stood up to very strong winds. With fifty metres of chain out and a
35lb CQR in fifteen metres of water it was something of a struggle to raise the
anchor a couple of times. An anchor windlass has been on the winter 'to do' list
for several years now. I made a mental note to winch it higher up the list.

Here at 68°28' north it was getting a tad chilly at night so I lit the charcoal
stove and gazed out through the
companionway at the vista of
snow capped peaks above the tree
clad slopes. Yes, tree clad slopes.
Anna had consulted an atlas and
found that one definition of the
Arctic is the northern limit of tree
growth. According to this
particular atlas the Arctic started

at 57° in Scotland and 70° in Norway. But we know that in Scotland the reason there's no trees in a lot of places is because, over the centuries, people have cut them down. So we've effectively, literally, created the Arctic in Scotland, whereas here, at 68°28′, two degrees inside the Arctic Circle, I'm still not far enough up to be in Arctic Norway.

I was in the mood for pondering further about life, the universe and everything. From the age of fourteen I have had a tendency to wander around listlessly daydreaming about all the adventures I might have travelling the world. Mostly these fantasies have been unlikely make-believe. I remember, long before I took up sailing, sitting on a remote beach in Sulawesi quizzing a guy supervising the building of a traditional Makassar ship about how much it would cost to buy one to sail the world in. The stuff of fantasy, it was never going to happen. It struck me suddenly that this was it. Here, deep in Arctic Norway I was having the adventure my fourteen year old self had idly dreamed of. This was living life and really, in practical terms, it didn't get any better than this. Apologies for the cliché, but I was 'living the dream'.

I'd decided this was going to be my furthest north. On the way some people – such as the German racist and Cap'n Vagrant - had said "what about going to Tromsø" and it was tempting. But if I went to Tromsø why would I not think "just one more little bit to Hammerfest" then it'd be the North Cape or Spitzbergen, then round the top of Spitzbergen or on to the Russian border and beyond. Things could get daft. 68°30′ north was quite enough in a 27ft tub, solo at four knots thank you very much. Besides which, I had run out of map. My paper charts stopped at 68°32′. At 68°33′ there be dragons.

North east Norway, before the Russian border, is further east than Istanbul. My furthest east didn't quite make Turkey, but I was as far east as Albania and a full hour east of Greenwich, That would do for this time.

For some random reason I decided I wanted to get to exactly 68.5 degrees, so motored a couple of miles further north to a point in the sea where my GPS confirmed that was how far north I was, then turned round and headed for home, with the Port Ed waypoint showing as 908 miles away bearing 221 degrees. I'd travelled 1405 miles from Port Ed to get there and was over an hour east of Greenwich. I'd been looking forward to the most northerly point and beginning the homeward journey, with the idea that on the way back I could

68°30′N

A wall. Well I thought it was nice

take it a lot easier and go slower. But I had mixed feelings at this ending, in a random bit of sea. It made me feel quite sad for some reason.

It also gave me quite a fright. Do you ever get Horizontal Vertigo? No? I suppose it ought to be called Hori*zon*tigo, probably with the emphasis on the 'zon'. Here's how you get it. Sail a small boat at four knots fourteen hundred miles in approximately the same direction. Do this with 1:50,000 charts and a chart plotter focussed in so that you can see no more than about five miles ahead all the way. Then, when you are at your furthest away from home, hit the 'Zoom Out' button on the chart plotter continually until you can see your home port in

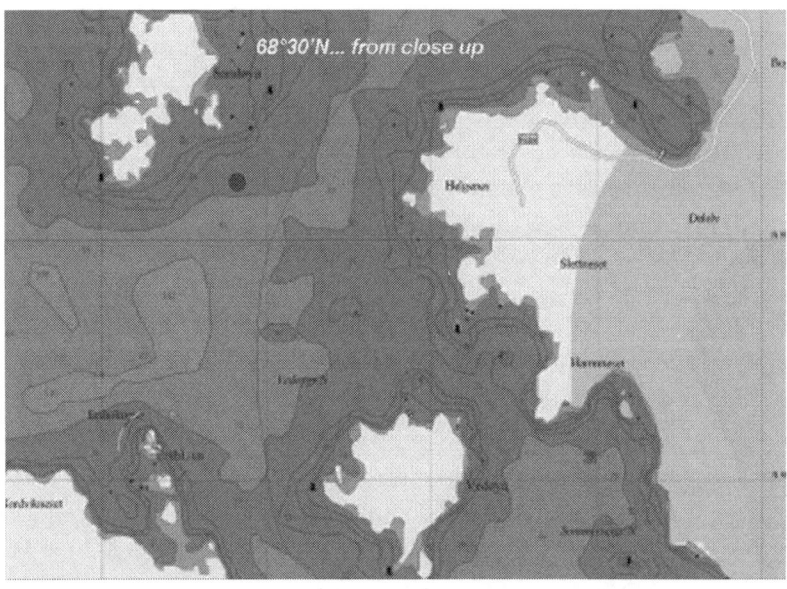

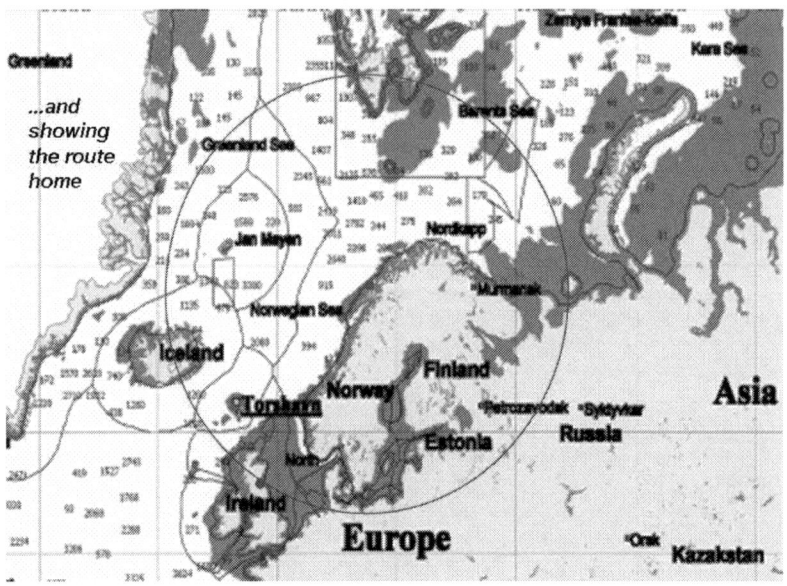

Britain. That's Horizontal Vertigo. There was no detail at all left on the chart at that scale. Just some shapes on the screen labelled 'Norway', 'Sweden', 'Iceland', 'Greenland', 'Russia' and 'UK', and some depth soundings around 2500 metres. You've to get back to Port Ed, at 4 knots, across what looks like half the planet.

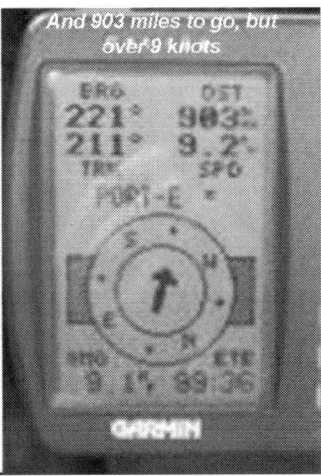

If you go climbing they say "don't look down", especially if you suffer from vertigo. If you're travelling a long way in a small boat, my advice is "don't look too far", if you don't want to get horizontigo.

Norwegian buoyage basically runs from south to north, so I'd been leaving green stuff to starboard and red stuff to port for three weeks. Now suddenly I had to shift my mindset to the opposite way around for the next three or four weeks. Distressingly, I had in effect to convert to the American IALA B buoyage system.

My GPS will only tell you how long it will take to get to your destination if it's less than a hundred hours. With the four knot tide down the Raftsund, by steering exactly 221° I was able to get the GPS to show an estimated time to Port Ed of 99 hours and 36 minutes. As long as we went in a dead straight line at 9.2 knots all the way. It was to be another month until I again saw an estimated trip time to Port Ed.

I had another squint into the Trollfjord on the way down, on the grounds that the weather was rather better now and I'd get better photos. Then it was on to Svolvær where I joined the queue to

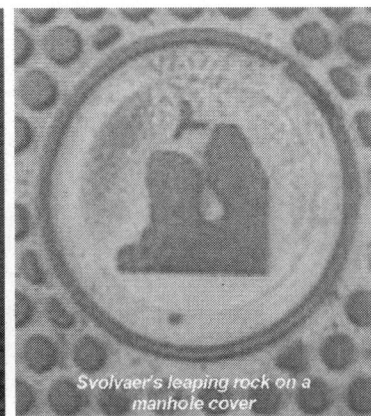

Svolvaer's leaping rock on a manhole cover

refuel in the marina at six p.m. on Friday night. Definitely rush hour. Then on to the rather more appealing town of Kabelvåg, where I tied to the incredibly sheltered pontoon outside the pub, just as, rather surreally, an oompah band was playing Auld Lang Syne.

Kabelvåg seemed to be in festival mood, with loads of stalls and a bouncy castle. Perhaps this was going to be their festival weekend. But no, as soon as I arrived the bouncy castle was deflated, all the stalls were removed and everyone buggered off, as did two of the three other visiting boats. Typical. I was just left with the increasingly pissed punters on the smoking balconies on the first floor of the pub looking straight down on me as I sat in the saloon drinking cans of beer from Tesco. I hope none of them were too distressed by the fact that I took another shower in my pesticide sprayer. I know I was overlooked but I was beginning to get a bit minging and the showering facilities were proving few and far between.

I went in search of midnight sun action. Aside from the wee peek I'd had in Bodø I really hadn't seen any actual midnight sun. Lofoten isn't really the best place to see the midnight sun. Don't get me wrong, it's better than, say Malaga, but it's not the best. The problem – apart from the fact that about half the nights had been cloudy - is that most of the time in the harbours of Lofoten you have a huge wall of mountains to the north of you. Kabelvåg wasn't quite as bad but I still didn't quite get to see the sun at midnight.

Everyone was going the other way

Flitting from Lofoten

The next day I left Lofoten on the relatively short crossing from Kabelvåg heading south east. Obviously Kabelvåg wasn't where the action was. I'd head south and see if there were more sailing boats down there. As the sun came out I got all sail up and motorsailed for a while. As the breeze from the north increased sailing became a possibility and the engine went off.

I saw another sail approaching from the south east. "At least someone else is out here, even if he is going in the opposite direction" I thought as a fast racing trimaran went past. I looked back to the south east. There were some dots on the horizon. In a rush they were upon me, a huge fleet of sailing boats of all kinds strung out as far as the eye could see. I lost count at a hundred boats. The trimaran was just leading the race. For the next three hours they went past. The modern cruiser-racers to windward of me, the tall ship, the old ketches, the few multihulls and the fleet of traditional Norwegian open boats with tan sails to leeward. I deduced from the fact that nobody was flying a flag (the Norgians are sticklers for flag etiquette) that this was probably a the race on a single tack from Bodø, perhaps having started about midnight.

Well over a hundred boats and not a single one was going the same way as me. Once I thought an old cutter was going my way, but he soon turned round and headed in the opposite direction. It was the story of my life. Both literally and metaphorically it seemed as though I was always sailing in the opposite direction to everyone else. Away

The following ten photos are all midnight sun porn...

...except this one

from where everything was happening. It always seemed to be the case when I travelled by bus around Asia, Africa and Central America. People would always ask, incredulously "but why are you going that way?". It usually seemed a sensible enough direction to me, but everyone else always seemed to know where the action was whilst I drifted around without a clue. But perhaps I'd been sailing too long solo and was beginning to get a little paranoid.

With the help of an increasing wind on the beam I soon reached the mainland side of the Vestfjord where I entered, once again, the Indreleia - the inside lane down the coast protected by islands and skerries. I sailed on, following an intricate course with some pretty nifty rock-dodging and changes in direction, though mostly on a dead run and often goose-winged in the sheltered, flat calm sections.

I realised something quite disturbing. If I got suitable winds, that is from somewhere in the north, the cockpit was going to be shaded from the sun by the sails practically the whole way home, as I sailed south. Bugger, I never thought of that.

The day was beautifully sunny but still chilly in the shade. I saw a sea eagle soaring over one of the wee islands we dodged round, then I sailed almost into the anchorage off a wee island in the Karlsøyvær archipelago, anchoring in ten metres, after a trip of 44 miles almost all under sail. I put a side anchor out to stop us drifting onto the island if the wind should come from the south. Though pretty sheltered the breeze swirled around the anchorage a bit, from all different directions.

There were small signs erected on the islands and islets round about. They appeared to say that these islands were a refuge for something and that landing was forbidden from April to July. I intended landing on an island to climb up and take a look at the midnight sun. Had I been caught in this activity on the deserted islands my defence would have been that I can't speak Norwegian and didn't understand the signs. But I did rather hope the islands were a refuge for meadow pipits or newts, not polar bears or wolves.

After about eleven p.m. the breeze died completely, I rowed out in the dinghy, landing on a small island and got some fantastic midnight sun action.

Absolutely beautiful.

A lot of people seem to think you are roughing it when staying on a small boat. I sat there in charcoal stove-heated toastiness in one of the planet's most idyllic spots. There was a bit of gentle rocking but no more than might have put a small sprog to sleep. Yes my home was quite small but it had a living room, study, bedroom, kitchen, dining room and bathroom - and just take a look outside. My view was of a maintenance free garden the size of the planet. There's a duck pond 3000 miles across and a rockery 5000 feet tall, behind which the lawn stretches to the other side of Siberia.

Of course the problem with the midnight sun is that it doesn't really make for very good pictures. It's just the sun, not a sunset, so it's just a big glare in the middle of the picture. But it does seem to make for some fantastic light effects. The cover photograph for this book, of a perfectly reflecting, calm sea and a beautiful sky, was taken from Zoph's cockpit that night.

At home we can describe the solstice quite simply. It's the shortest night. How do you do it here, when for weeks there is no night? I suppose it's the night when the sun, at its lowest point that day, is the highest it gets at the lowest point, if you see what I mean. You don't? No, I'm not sure I do either.

Though the next day was supposed to bring a stiff force four or five, actually I saw bugger all wind as I motored through the Indreleia on a straightforward course with few changes of direction. Zoph rolled a lot with the gentle swell from the north as I headed south west. I should have put the mainsail up to limit the rolling but frankly I couldn't be bothered. There was little traffic, with a few folk out fishing and a couple of yachts, but very quiet for a Sunday, even as I went past busy Bodø. I tied to the guest pontoon in another fantastically sheltered harbour in the middle of the island of Stott. Another one where you

have to do several 180° turns to get in. I was later told that just before arriving in Stott I'd traversed one of Norway's fabled area of 'dangerous waves'. I can't say I noticed.

In Støtt I had what I realised was my first real shower (as opposed to pesticide spray shower), for twelve days. One shower a fortnight, what's wrong with that? I also cooked the next day's dinner on my leccy stove in the cockpit. This consisted of a whole chicken pot roasted. The chicken was too big for my largest pan so was forced into it with a large tower of weights holding the lid on as it simmered for about five hours. The reason for this eccentric behaviour was the differential cost of foodstuffs in Norway. I practically couldn't afford to eat chicken, as a small fillet cost over a tenner. It was possible, however, to find one brand of whole frozen chicken that cost a bout two quid. A whole frozen chicken was also quite a useful boost for Zoph's well insulated but power-hungry fridge, given the dodgy state of the batteries and the lack of ice in the shops.

This need to cook eccentrically large amounts of the same foodstuff didn't stop at chicken. The other two things that were cheap were pork chops and salmon fillets. However they only came in packs of at least four, so I had to try and think of different things to do with the same stuff four nights running. It wasn't that these things were marginally cheaper than other things. A bit of salmon would cost about one or two quid. A wee bit of stewing beef was about fifteen quid. This fact, coupled to the extremely high prices in the most greasy spoon of 'restaurants', did lead to a somewhat monotonous diet. It was a bit frustrating to buy Norwegian stuff out of Norwegian shops, yet to know that I was just cooking stuff as I would have done at home. The whole summer I had no real sense of exploring any Norwegian cuisine.

In Støtt, which had a washing machine, I also washed a pile of clothes for the first time. These I hung on a washing line which I strung all round a humiliated Zoph. I moved her along the pontoon a bit to get out of the shade of a building and left the clothes to dry overnight in the midnight sun. And they did. They were hung up at eleven p.m. and dry by Seven a.m..

Støtt provided more fantastic midnight sun action that night, this time with possibly the best rainbow I have ever seen, reflected in a still harbour pool to make a perfect circle, just after the sun was at its lowest point. I Brompted around the island at night, trying ineffectually to capture the extraordinary light effects with my camera.

That midnight - and the rainbow - heralded the start of the last day of June and my birthday. At 51 it wasn't a particularly significant birthday, unless you think of three times seventeen as an important number. I suppose on that birthday I had been legally entitled to drive for two thirds of my life, but that's clutching at straws.

For my birthday the Norges had laid on a proper hot summer's day the next morning, with full sun and, for once, temperatures warm enough that you were grateful for a bit of shade. But I was a man with a mission – a quest if you will - and I needed to get to a glacier.

I motored the twenty miles or so to Engen, on the Hollandsfjord, where you can tie to a pontoon and Brompt, walk and climb, to what is apparently the lowest arm of a glacier on mainland Europe, at only 170m above sea level. It was another place I'd visited briefly before on Equinox, but well worth another look. I took a rucksack and a hammer and cycled, walked and struggled up the rocks. The views are magnificent, but of course as soon as I reached the top the battery on my camera went flat, which happens without warning.

I didn't want to stay at Engen as the wind was predicted to increase and go round to the south west, which could be uncomfortable on the exposed pontoon. Back at the boat after a couple of hours on land I tried sailing for a bit – something for the boatloads of touros to look at – then gave up and motored to the harbour and the small boat club moorings in the village of Halsa.

This was another unbelievably sheltered natural harbour, almost certainly better than anything we've got in Britain, yet unremarkable and commonplace here. The wee club house was a proper little house. It had a lounge with sofas and bookshelves and a telly, a fully equipped kitchen with coffee and biscuits and a bathroom. All open twenty four hours a day for the use of those paying the fee of eight quid a boat for the night.

For the first time since Hardbakke, just north of Bergen, it was warm enough to sit out in a tee shirt at night, so I ate my posh birthday dinner of broiled-to-bits chicken on deck, using my new cockpit table for the first time. As I ate my dinner the motor boat from Tromsø I'd seen in Henningsvær showed up and moored next to Zoph.

Oh and of course I had Svartisen ice for my birthday G&T. My glacier-related quest having been successful.

Svartisen: Designed to support the G&T industry

Later a Norgian couple moored just behind Zoph in a motorboat from Bodø invited me on board and fed me Talisker single malt. It probably cost them about sixty quid a bottle here. I shamefacedly told him that all I had was Bert's North Sea Whisky, at £3.50 a litre.

The next day was remarkable in that I didn't go anywhere. It was July 1st and the first day Zoph had not moved since May 28th. Well it was pretty miserable and dreich. I changed the oil and did stuff like that.

I did go for a walk and see and owl though. It was flying about in broad daylight. Then it struck me that the poor bugger doesn't have much choice in the land of the midnight sun. I wonder how they survive through the several months a year when it doesn't get properly dark and the field mice and what have you can see them coming perfectly clearly. It must be a right pain in the arse.

The other bird species I felt sorry for was the herons. There seemed to be loads of them about in Norway and as you know a heron's preferred modus operandum is to stand about knee deep in water until a fish saunters along. There's plenty of fish in Norway but bugger all bits of sea that are knee deep. Typically Norway is divided into land and deep sea, with very little in the way of shallows. The few bits of sea with just-submerged rocks have generally got a stick or some other navigation mark on them. Heron loitering points must be thin on the ground and quite sought after.

Apart from owls and the herons, the other wildlife worthy of note here is midges. The previous year I was struck by how lucky the southern Norgians seemed to be, as I didn't notice a single midge. There had been one or two on occasion since Bergen, but here, on a dampish and warm night, though by no means of scary west coast of Scotland proportions, the midge menace is just about enough to drive you indoors. I hoped I'd lose them as I headed south.

I wandered around Halsa. An unremarkable place in many ways, with a strung out population of perhaps 100, until you realise how much activity there is. This is the middle of nowhere remember, with a tiny population. The marina has forty two fully occupied pontoon spaces. There are two supermarkets, one quite large (Shetland, with a population of 23,000, has only 1), a B&Q style builders' merchant, a hotel, a café, a large garage doing major repair work, a factory making wooden palettes from local materials, a huge fishing boat (ship, really) with its own dock and processing facilities and another large factory, making god knows what, with its own ship dock. In terms of transport a large car ferry goes over to a tiny peninsula with bugger all population. There are fifteen sailings each way a day all winter, more in summer.

The amount of spread-out economic activity in all these wee places is truly incredible. Halsa was not unusual, it is the norm, even north of the Arctic Circle. Every village in Norway seems to have industry, retail and ferry links. Not all of this is paid for out of oil taxes. The wee factories are successful independent businesses which seem to work despite the sky-high wage bills and taxes. How they manage it I don't know, but the Norges have certainly got something right about running small economies.

After a one day damp aberration the next dawned utterly sunny and I headed off under a full sun and full sail on a reach at up to 6.6 knots. As I moved round onto a dead run the speed dropped, but the whole day was spent under full sail, goose winged or on a broad reach, with the staysail going up and down four or five times as I moved from a run to a reach. I bade goodbye to the Arctic and looked forward to some semblance of darkness as an incentive to getting to bed at a reasonable hour.

I had looked forward to getting to the land of the midnight sun but even long before I arrived in the Arctic I could appreciate the downside. I'm not a very early-to-bed person at the best of times and when it really doesn't get dark at all I found it particularly difficult. When the sun was actually up all night it was even worse. Night after night I would think it was about ten p.m. and be constantly, ludicrously surprised to see that it was actually three a.m.

When I asked Norwegians how they managed they all told me that they just get used to it. Observation over time suggested that this was patently crap. It  only happens for a month or two a year and they clearly have never got used to it. This is particularly evident amongst the sprogs. All summer hyperactive Norgian children are rampaging about the villages and harbours after midnight, their parents obviously having completely lost control of them. I was reminded that we are a species which evolved high above sea level on the equator. We are designed for a steady diurnal rhythm. We are not polar bears designed for an annual rhythm of hibernation and twenty four hour wakefulness. I suspect prolonged exposure to the far north drives you a bit mad.

I needed the engine for a couple of miles, first as I passed the misplaced so called self styled 'Arctic Monument' and again to pass round the bottom of Handnesøy Island. At times Zoph dropped down to three knots, but I resolutely kept sailing all day to N.E.S.N.A, the first place on my itinerary I'd visited twice.

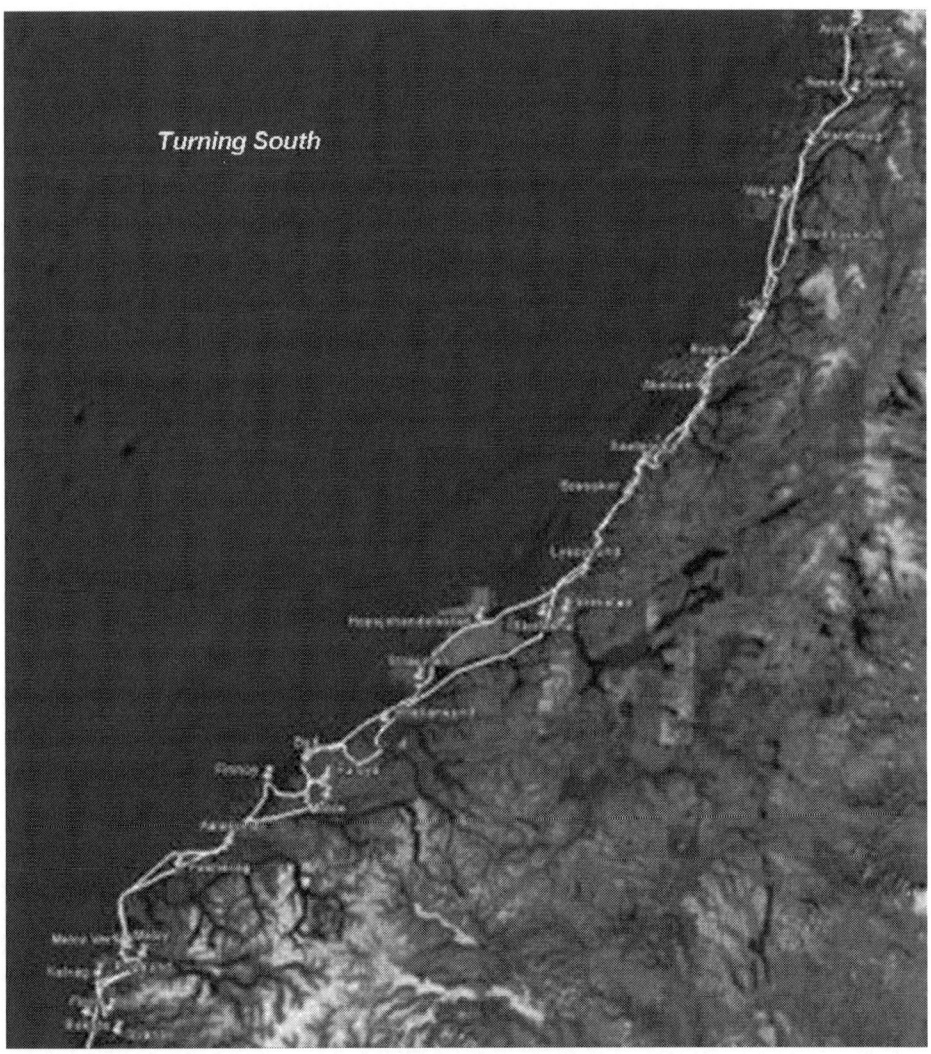

Out of the Arctic

My chum the harbour master – actually one of a group of blokes in the sailing club who take it in turns to take money from visitors – spotted me and I was persuaded on board his now floating boat for a beer. We were joined by his mate, a Walter Mathau look-alike. They consumed quantities of crab and crab eggs they'd caught the previous autumn, then Walter stuck a wad of chewing tobacco under his top lip as we partook of a beer. I saw a few blokes chewing tobacco in Norway and it wasn't always the octogenarians. It's a habit that's persisted probably about seventy years after the last British chewer was buried.

Later I was persuaded into a boozer for a beer – the first booze bought in a pub since Lerwick. The bar was a sort of conical hut in a caravan site. Though it looked very much like it was just there for the holiday season, I was assured that it operated all year and was a big hit with the students in the local teacher training college. Of course a town with a population of a thousand or so had to have a university.

My chum's wife was apparently away in London so he was making strenuous efforts to chat up a 60 year old bint with dyed red hair, who was quite far gone by the time I got there and well pissed by the time, back on his boat, the cognac appeared at 2 am. She was utterly incredulous that anyone would choose to sail this far in a small boat. I pointed out that, whilst I expected such incredulity from people in Britain who thought northern Norway was just icebergs and polar bears, she should know better, as she saw all the wee open boats out fishing in the perfectly sheltered waters.

Walter Mathau appeared to be something of a Britophyle and was off on holiday to North Wales in a week or so. Looking at the snow covered peaks all around us it struck me that he might feel that the name Snowdonia was something of a letdown. The Welsh tourist Board doubtless presents it as a majestic mountain wilderness, but if you were used to this landscape it'd feel more like Norfolk.

Walt had been all over Britain, including Stornoway and other bits of Scotland. When I asked about my next destination, the World Heritage island of

The name 'Svartisen' means 'son of Slartibartfast'

The Arctic Circle

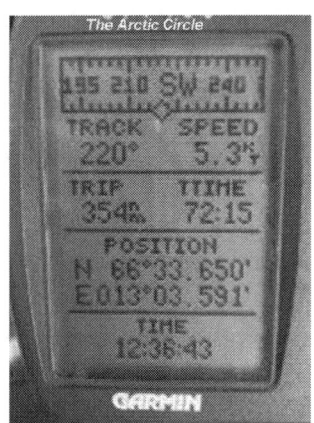

The Arctic Circle

TRACK
220°

SPEED
5.3k

TRIP
354m

TTIME
72:15

POSITION
N 66°33.650'
E 013°03.591'

TIME
12:38:43

GARMIN

...and the Norwegian monument to it several miles away

Vega, some forty miles further on, I was somewhat surprised that none of the three of them had ever been there.

The machinations of the Harbour Master as he tried to inveigle his way into the affections of the old bint with the dyed hair became something of an embarrassment to both me and Walt, so I retired to drunken choruses of 'I love you, you're my best mate you are' and the like.

Another beautiful day dawned and when I could sail at over 3.5 knots I did so. Most of it was on a broad reach or a dead run goose winged. The wind died at times and the jib was furled and unfurled about ten times, the staysail and the main went up and down twice.

The reason the main came down was that I diverted into Alstahaug, home of the apparently famous poet Peter Dass. Of Scottish descent, he was a big cheese in Norway in the 17th century. The tiny little hamlet with a wee church and a couple of houses had, of course, a massive modern architectural excrescence which was the Peter Dass museum. Round about as big an undertaking as the Museum of Scotland in Edinburgh, this one was in the middle of nowhere and its exhibits were just about one bloke. The amount of money sloshing around in Norway is truly mind boggling.

The wee bit of pontoon space was full however so I carried on to Vega, where I tied up in the predictably picture postcard perfect harbour. Another minor milestone as I'd done over a thousand miles solo in Norway since leaving Hjellestad after Ian left. Vega is a large mountainous island, but the bit where I was – and the main settlements were – was quite a flat offshoot of the main

lump of rock. I headed off on the
Brompt with my camera, past
Hebridean landscapes, seemingly
hundreds of narrow sea channels
wandering through the low rocky
landscape, past lush green fields and
prosperous farms, past perfect
holiday hamlets crowded round
perfect, still, natural harbours.

The Peter Dass Museum (the big thing at the back)

I cycled at some speed since I was
beset by flies. Not midges but proper
flies of the corks-round-the-brim-of-the-hat-in-the-outback variety. They could
only fly at about eight knots and swarmed round my unwashed form. When I
looked behind me I could see a great phalanx of them following me like a swarm
of cartoon bees. If I accelerated to around twelve knots I would lose them for a
while, but as soon as I slowed down they, or a related swarm, came at me again.

I stopped to take a photo and the flies were swarming all over me so much
that, in slapping them off, I only succeeded in flinging the camera, with some
force, down into the tarmac. This had the effect, predictably enough, of breaking
it and causing it to give error messages every time I turned it on. Bugger. Two
cameras destroyed in four weeks.

Vega has a museum established and run by the local community. Inevitably
it was shut when I was there, but apparently it's open during the summer
season. It's telling that it turns out the summer season consists of the month of
July. The museum is open five days a week until four p.m. for one month only.
Everywhere I see reminders that this fantastic summer idyll the Norgians live is
in fact very short lived indeed.

I did see a boat registered in Vega, with the port of registration printed after
the name on the stern. It read 'Susanne, Vega'. I hope it was a joke

Every day when I arrived in a new place I texted Anna to let her know
where I was. 'Vega' was easy, but places like Henningsvær were a bugger with
predictive text, so I decided to stick with short names and simple spellings. A
poor rationale for planning a passage perhaps, but it was at least a plan. Hence
the island of Leka was to be my next port of call.

Another beautiful day and I set off under motor for a couple of hours, then
goose-winged it slowly on a rolly sea, then had a decent reach. The wind was
fickle in strength and direction however and I sometimes had to motor, sailing
on the reaches and when the wind was strongest.

There were a couple of boats on the long pontoon when I tied up in Leka.
The one ahead of me was occupied by a friendly Norwegian couple who had
sailed to Scotland. A free tourist leaflet I'd picked up before suggested that there
was a shop nearby, open until eight. I asked the bloke where the shop was and

he told me, explaining that it would be shut now but open at ten a.m.. I thanked him and got on my Brompt. "HELLO!" he shouted as if to someone very hard of understanding "THE SHOP IS SHUT NOW, O-P-E-N I-N T-H-E M-O-R-N-I-N-G!" "Yes, thank you, I'm just going for a bike ride" I said, not wanting to seem to be ignoring his advice. I returned an hour later laden down with bags of shopping, the shop having been open until eight as I predicted. I rubbed his face in the shopping a little bit. Metaphorically, you understand.

Vega

When a chunky old Hallberg Rassy 35 arrived later its skipper decided to go onto a small finger pontoon. Intending to go port side to, onto the leeward pontoon in the increasingly strong breeze, he tied fenders only to the starboard, windward side and attached no lines. He approached the incredibly wobbly and narrow pontoon at full pelt, relying on my body to act as a fender, since I'd offered to help. Once he'd hit and I was struggling both to balance and fend him off, he sauntered to the bow to attach an utterly pointless lee side bow rope. I protested at the lack of fenders and eventually one was called for.

I suggested that he tie the boat off to windward, which he eventually agreed to. Having little concept of springs he dispatched me up the tiny, wobbly, windward side pontoon, against which there was no boat to balance. Having nearly fallen in a couple of times I resorted to crawling back to safety, which induced much hilarity amongst the onlookers.

Norwegians have no concept of controlling and shortening lines from the boat, so my line, attached to the pontoon with a fine bowline at huge personal risk to me, sat limply trailing in the water all night while the boat scraped up and down on the pontoon.

My Norwegian language pilot, in its wee English section, describes Leka as having 'remarkable species of rock'. Apparently it's part of the Caledonian

One of the legendary winking houses of Leka

range and strongly linked in geological history to Scotland. How this one island – and not all the bits in between – can be part of a set of Scottish mountains, you'll have to ask a geologist.

The next day was again, as was so often the case, totally sunny, but this time with increasingly strong, though favourable, wind. I was heading to Villa, in Flatanger. Flatanger is an administrative district and not, as you might suppose, a sort of rage induced by being in an apartment. Villa was my choice for the obvious reason that it had a name that was easy to text. I had a gentle reach for a while then a fast reach under full sail, when a texted forecast from Anna suggested that I could expect winds increasing to force seven from the north east. The approaches south of Rørvik, which I'd have to cross to get to Villa, are another area with 'dangerous waves' written all over the chart and, despite the fact that it's south westerlies that present the real problems, I decided to cut my journey short at the rather less spelling friendly Abelvær.

I sailed under the bridge past Rørvik against a couple of knots of tide, then tucked in a couple of reefs to sail through the narrow and twisting channels south east of Rørvik. Eventually, with the wind gusting to 20 to 25 knots true, I sailed down a particularly narrow bit of channel right into the sheltered harbour in Abelvær. As I did so I briefly wondered whether it was really a big enough channel for a boat the size of Zoph. Predictably, at that moment a ruddy great hydrofoil ferry with a hundred passengers zoomed out at full speed. Abelvær is perfectly sheltered natural harbour three hundred metres across which the Norgians have, of course, spend a few million quid building a causeway across, because three hundred metres is like the open ocean and they wanted the harbour to be one hundred metres across.

I tied to the last wee pontoon space in the blustery and busy wee harbour. It was Sunday and there was a real holiday atmosphere about the place. Obviously a popular spot amongst Rørvikians. You could see why as once again the views were predictably beautiful and the wee houses and streets painfully twee.

I had thought I was on an island and this seemed to be confirmed by the constant stream of ferries. But no – on looking at the chart I saw there was a string of bridges leading back to the mainland and Rørvik. But still there's a load of ferries going there. Unlike in Scotland the sea remains a major thoroughfare.

I had a quick Brompt through the tweenery to an apparently famous monument – a burial mound of some old Viking bloke. Just a small green hill with a picnic table on top. The sign said it had never been excavated. There's not much physical evidence of very old history in Norway and a definite paucity of old castles and the like. A consequence, of course, of building everything in wood.

By eleven p.m. as I sat on board, two sprogs, aged about six and nine, still rowed backwards and forwards across the harbour and out into more open water, a contented species of marine mammal whose parents, in their wee gin palace at the other end of the harbour, were nowhere to be seen. It was a rare sprog in Norway who would be satisfied with a pair of oars in lieu of an outboard motor.

The predictive text problem became horrific the next day as I headed off in the sun with twenty knots of breeze on the beam to Sætervika, via Hamnvika, Kvernøya, Viksfjorden, Kvaloya and Bulholmrasa. After sailing with two reefs in the main the short ten mile crossing of the feared Folda – another bit with 'dangerous waves' written all over the chart – I took the wimp's route in the

strong winds – peaking about force six - sailing the long way round through tortuous channels, past low rocky islands and high, steep mountains.

As I negotiated the narrower bits or the wind dropped in the shelter of headlands the jib

...and the shy houses of Bulholmrasa

was furled, coming out again for the breezier bits. In all it was furled and unfurled about ten times. Eventually I emerged and sailed round another famously exposed bit, the lighthouse at Bulholmrasa, where a five foot swell – surprisingly from the north west, where the wind had not been coming from – showed that this was a real bit of sea and could probably get rough at times.

Lysoysund

There were a couple of visiting sailing boats on the pontoon at Sætervika, just past the lighthouse, but plenty of room for Zoph. The village – a popular holiday spot of course – was completely dominated by Germanglers zapping about in dented aluminium speedboats rented along with the wooden hut accommodation. It seems to be a slightly annoying German trait to hang German national flags on the stern of these boats, even though the boats, if not the occupants, are clearly Norwegian.

You will be unsurprised to learn that the next day was sunny as I sailed in a gusty easterly, in full sail down the complex Indreleia, then into more open, but still sheltered waters. The wind was up to 25kt and down to five knots in a matter of seconds. So even in the smooth sea I managed to give the decks a wash occasionally as Zoph heeled to the gusts. Near the steeper headlands seemed to be the worst, with the wind backing and increasing to push Zoph over. It was, however, an exhilarating, if sometimes frustrating and tiring day's sailing, with speeds of up to seven knots.

Towards the end of the passage I passed down the mile wide channel between the Stokkøya and the outer island of Linesøya, where no bridge was shown on the chartplotter, despite Linesøya having a population of almost a hundred. I didn't recognise some of the buoyage and realised, of course, that they were busy building a bridge. Huge causeways built of mammoth rocks stretched out from either side of the channel sweeping upwards at the end in curves which would eventually culminate in a two hundred metre wide bridge at

The guest harbour at Lysoysund

least twenty metres high. After all you couldn't expect the Linesøyans to get a ferry. It must have been costing at least a million quid per inhabitant. At least.

I tucked in a couple of reefs to go to windward down this channel, then down Linesfjorden to the visitors' pontoon at Lysøysund, where I joined a Norgian yacht, a big old wooden boat and a crowd of happy, noisy folk, featuring teenagers in speedboats creating a lot of rather annoying wash.

The pilot book spoke of the redundant, closed down fish packing factory at Lysøysund and indeed it was a landmark for several senses from quite a long way away. Fortunately for some, but unfortunately for me and the other tourists, it had not closed down, but stank of rotting fish, as did the whole of Lysøysund. Other than that, which you can, I suppose, get used to in time, it was a jolly, sunny, green place with a holiday atmosphere.

It was another sunny day as I left under engine dressed, distressingly for any onlookers, in shorts and no shirt. At first I thought I'd not get a sail as there wasn't enough wind, but I hoisted the main anyway. I'd decided to sail a different route southwards to the one I'd taken going north, round the north side of large Hitra island, where there were good sheltered channels and I'd been told yet more lovely scenery. Soon I was sailing on a broad reach with a steady twenty knots apparent. I tucked in a couple of reefs and lowered the staysail as I left the shelter of Tarva Island and soon we were surfing down choppy five foot waves in increasingly strong winds and rising seas. The highest speed I saw on the GPS was 9.6 knots as we crossed the open water, seemingly the only boat at sea. Leo the autohelm steered well as we shot across the open water on a broadish reach.

Back in the shelter of the narrow Dolmøysund after two or three hours the wind became much more fickle and variable, but also less, so I shook out the reefs and sailed on. We passed houses and holiday homes lining both sides of the sound, a caravan site and a holiday complex. Then, right next to the holiday caravans, a huge shipyard, with ships of all kinds from all over Norway and the rest of Northern Europe moored up awaiting repair. Ferries and tankers and ocean-going tugs. All sorts. It seems OK in Norway to mix heavy industry in remote rural areas with tourism. It wouldn't work in Scotland, but somehow the Norwegians have got it

The appallingly named Hopsjø Handelssted

right.

I sailed quietly under a narrow bridge with two knots of tide in my favour and arrived at the pontoon of the disastrously named Hopsjø Handelssted. I tied up on the huge new hundred metre long concrete pontoon behind, for once, a smaller cruising boat than Zoph – a 26 footer bought north of Tromsø and now being sailed home to somewhere in the south by a young couple. The bloke asked if I was staying the night there. I said I was. He explained that this huge pontoon was not the guest harbour, but just the waiting pontoon belonging to the small Co-op shop in the village. Basically it was the car park for the wee Spar shop and the place where all the speedboats tie up to do the weekly shopping. It was a bigger and more substantial pontoon than any pontoon anywhere in the Forth.

I moved into the real guest harbour, which was attached to a pub round the corner. At least I tried to. With the wind blowing off the pontoon I made several attempts while a couple of folk – unusually for Norway, just looked on and didn't offer to help. Eventually I made a death-defying leap ashore and struggled to tie her on. Once I'd completely finished and required no further help an old manny tottered over from a wee motorboat and offered to help.

It was mid afternoon and aside from the old manny's boat the place was deserted. I assumed it'd fill up later when the pub hotted up. After all, in a tiny rural holiday place like this, the pub really only had the holiday season of July to make any money.

At 6 pm precisely the pub shut and everyone went home. Leaving just me and the old manny. This was a recurrent theme for me in Norway. How was it possible that these businesses –apparently shut for ninety percent of the time even at the peak of the high season – hadn't gone bankrupt? Where were all the thousands of people I saw by day whizzing around in their little speedboats? Above all, WHY WAS THE PUB SHUT!

As I walked around exploring the village I was accosted by an old mad woman, eccentrically swathed from head to toe in dirty white robes. Though apparently a Norwegian, it came as no surprise when this apparition told me she lived in America for half the year. She explained to me that, even though she lived in America, she was entitled to criticise Bush's war in the Middle East because she was a Norwegian citizen. The implication, of course, was that were she an American citizen she would have no right to criticise her Government's policies. I suspected that, insane though this may seem, she was probably right in the eyes of Americans. I continued with my rather depressed wander, pondering on the nature of democracy and freedom of speech, if any, in America.

Heading for the Deep South

I had a change from the monotony of endless hot sun as the next day was cloudy and slightly dreich, with little or no wind. It was primarily a day for just motoring to get somewhere. I did get a gentle reach at up to four knots for a short while, in company with the wee yacht from the Co-op, but soon the jib was furled and I motored on ahead.

The narrow channels that skirt the northern edge of Hirta were awash with Germanglers speeding around or angling away. When I see open boats out in the open sea I always assume they are locals and must know what they are doing. If it's a bit rough and windy I think I must be incredibly wimpy to have any anxieties about the passage in an ocean-going yacht while there's open boats about. I was later told however that a lot of these open boats are tourists – mostly Germen – and that there's a significant problem with drowning Germen. They've booked their fishing holiday and they're sodding well going fishing, however dangerous and even if there is a hurricane.

There was no particular danger that day however, as I threaded my way down the flat calm lanes in the drizzle. Coming out into the open there was a slight swell from the north before I entered yet more sheltered channels around the island of Smølla and tied up on the guest pontoon at Straumen.

I always find it difficult to interpret what a place is really like from a pilot or a guidebook. I hadn't expected Straumen to feel as though Zoph was the first boat ever to visit and tie up amongst the few wee open fishing boats. There were supposed to be washing facilities and I asked in the local library next to the pontoons where they were. The librarian had no idea there were such facilities. I eventually discovered that they were the other half of the bungalow that contained the library. This rather did suggest that nobody had every used these facilities before.

Another night wondering – in a rather paranoid way – where everybody was and why I was the only one not at the party. Still, I got the key to the toilets, shower, washing machine and tumble drier and did some much needed ablutions. The building had the world's strongest shower, which was also free. The shower cubicle was heated by an electric panel heater plugged in just above floor level directly in the line of fire of the shower. It was an electric element

Norway's answer to Eddie Grundy

completely doused every time the shower was switched on. I made certain the bloody thing wasn't plugged in, but it still made me nervous. There's some pretty dodgy electrical and plumbing arrangements in some Norwegian bog-blocks.

Whilst I had been pottering gently round Hirta to Straumen I began to realise that, given the forecast, the next day was likely to be the only real opportunity for a while to thread my way back through the exposed and tortuous Hustadvika. The wind was due to increase to force six or more in the evening, so in the morning I sped off with alacrity at 8.30. About a mile or so out I sped back again to return the bog key, not wishing to add it to my burgeoning collection. Not a good start.

It was with mixed feelings that I sped away from the island of Smølla, which has around it some of the most spectacularly complex and dodgy rocky channels in the whole of Norge. I had half considered trying to negotiate a few of them. The 1:50,000 Admiralty chart of the waters round Smølla is just pale blue with the legend 'Dangerous Shoals' written all over it and a first look at the chartplotter appears to confirm that diagnosis. At a scale of 1:150,000 Smølla looks like a snow storm has hit it. Hundreds of white dots litter the screen. They are rocks and there would appear to be no way through them.

At a scale of 1:50,000 it looks even worse. It's like a hyperactive child has been let loose with a felt pen and had a veritable orgy of scribbling black dots and marks all over the chart. It's an utterly impenetrable mess of rocks. Go in further however and at a scale of 1:12,500 a series of wiggly black lines appears between the rocks. These are official channels – some of them marked by red and green sticks – through the kind of sea that no sane British sailor would ever consider navigating. A large part of me was grateful not to have the opportunity to explore further.

I raised the main in the force two wind from astern but I'm afraid motored at

six knots to beat the weather window. The breeze was due to begin increasing round the Hustadvika in the afternoon, reaching force six from offshore by four pm. This time I took the outer route past Kristiansund and the 'Atlantic Road', rejoining my 'past track' on the computer chart for the more exposed bit of the Hustadvika, where the pilotage would be exceedingly difficult without a chart plotter. I really was getting lazy at navigation as I just steered Zoph back over the wee black dots on the screen marking my outward route.

Though there were few boats at first, I was joined through the maze by a traditional open boat - which I overtook - and a big Swedish motor-sailer – which overtook me. Following the Swedes seemed to be an unreliable course of action as on at least one occasion they wandered off on entirely the wrong course away from the channel and had to pick their way back through the rocks.

The Norwegian Met Office at www.yr.no gives detailed forecasts for everywhere in Norway with a name. I'd pick somewhere nearby and exposed to the sea where possible and get regularly updated forecasts if I was navigating anywhere at all dodgy. Anna had sent me an hour by hour forecast for a small exposed island not far away and as predicted the breeze started up at about three p.m. It was a north easterly, which was perfect, but I didn't fancy doing the difficult Hustadvika pilotage in open waters with waves crashing on rocks all about with strong winds from any direction.

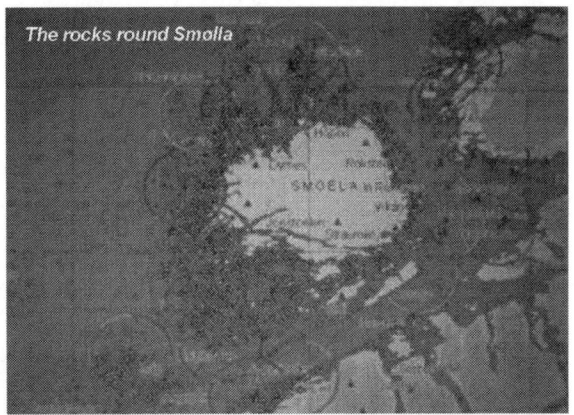

The rocks round Smolla

By four p.m. the wind had risen to a force five and as I tied up in the one remaining space on the guest pontoon at Bud, it continued to rise, so that by ten p.m. it was blowing a good force seven. Good fortune remained with me and the timing was perfect. A side effect of the rising wind was that it blew all the low cloud away, giving a sunny evening in a chill breeze.

More boats continued to arrive – from the south hoping to find another Hustad-window, as well as from the north. A huge British yacht sailed past from the north and anchored in the next bay. A sloop, it had

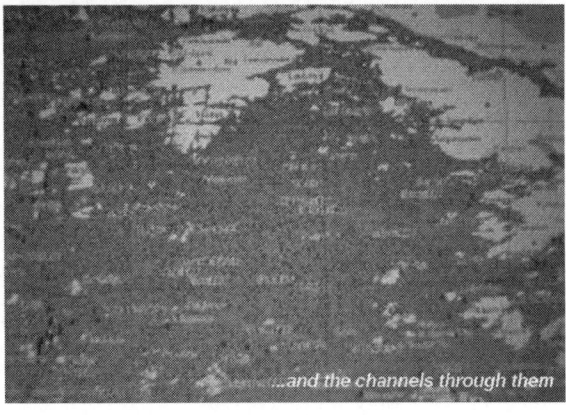

...and the channels through them

one less sail than Zoph carries, yet was the sort of size that seemed to demand at least three masts and four jibs. That night the eight or so assorted boats against the pontoon all had either one or two boats rafted up against them. Except, of course, Zoph. Too wee and too

A tight squeeze getting out of the harbour at Molde

One of the many hotels in Molde, population 18,000

foreign, she had a huge space to herself. Though this is clearly a good thing, my perverse mind did manage to wonder if we smelled or had leprosy. I was almost relieved when, the next morning, a larger Danish yacht rafted up on Zoph, albeit only for a couple of hours.

Incredibly, I found bags of ice in one of the supermarkets in Bud, bought one and put it in the fridge to give it a helping hand. At least I think I did. When I went back to the shop for more the following morning there was no sign of ice or even a gap in the freezer cabinet or a price tag where it had been. Back at the boat a leaky bag of cold water in the fridge was inconclusive evidence that ice had ever existed.

It was still blowing about a force six that morning and I thought I had a good few days to go the next sixty miles or so to the dreaded Stad peninsula (the one that *'sticks out like an angrily clenched fist'* you'll remember), since the forecast suggested I'd need to wait a while for another good weather window. So I had a lazy morning then in the afternoon sailed on a fast reach in the sun under jib only to the town of Molde, where there was reputed to be

Bud

a jazz festival starting up. Happily it wasn't starting for a couple of days so I wouldn't have to listen to it, but the build-up and the throng of boats might be jolly. I'd expected the north east wind to head me when I turned east, but for once Sod's law didn't apply and whenever I had to change course round a headland the wind shifted to keep us on a nice broad reach or a run.

The pilot book said that Molde harbour was 'mostly for local motor boats', but that a yacht under twelve metres might find a space. As I arrived I passed the huge British yacht I'd seen the night before – Dream Catcher – tied to the outside of the visitors' pontoon. I hailed the folk on board and said that I had seen few British boats in Norway. 'Excuse me sir?', they all said, every man-jack of them a bleedin' American. The next time I was to see her was later that year, towards the end of December. She was sitting in the marina in St Lucia as I arrived across the Atlantic aboard Equinox. In the meantime, inside Molde harbour was hooching with motor boats, many of them huge million pound plus gin palaces and not a local boat in sight, nor much - other than Zoph - that was less than 12m.

I rafted up on a small Bavaria, nose to tail and facing outwards for an easy getaway. I was told by the Bavaria's occupants that the rule in this harbour was that all boats had to face in the same direction, 'in case of fire' apparently. I still can't work that one out. I decided to ignore the rule on the grounds that I was a stupid foreigner who spoke neither Norwegian nor English and was hard of understanding.

I know I keep going on about it but Norway was creaking and groaning under an immense weight of money. The pilot book claims that Molde has a population of 18,000. It has a brand new sports stadium which must be the equal of anything in Britain. We've probably got ones with greater capacity, but where else would you find a brand new five storey football stadium clad entirely, from top to toe and all round, in polished granite. The tiny wee town also has an emblematic new hotel, A high spiky tower designed by an Architect with a small penis which looked like it belonged in Sydney harbour or somewhere – the iconic structure for a major world capital.

At night an ageing pop star started crooning at huge volume over the marina. I was told that this was one of Norway's biggest stars from the seventies. Once he sang protest songs but now sings about love and mortgages to an audience of £1 million Princess 48 gin palaces. God knows how he'll make any money because there was absolutely no reason to pay for his concert. You could see and hear it perfectly well from anywhere on land or afloat. Indeed quite a number of fans turned up in wee speed boats and just bobbed about in the harbour, without tying onto anything, for much of the gig. Can you imagine such a thing in Britain? All the fans turning up to an open air concert in speed boats. Norway in the summer is the most surreal country.

The Hurtigrute ships travelling both north and south dock in Molde in quick succession and I wandered over to see one of them discharge its cargo of primarily east Asian tourists. As its lines were thrown ashore two huge doors in its side began an automated ballet of complicated movements as doors swung slowly up, ramps slowly down, steps slowly outwards, handrails upwards and sideways. It was like a CGI space station opening up to allow its scout ships out. Down the steps and ramps hundreds of mostly amiable, grinning touros streamed for their half hour exploring the streets of Molde. As they did so they were greeted by the deafening tones of the old crooner blasting out a song in Norwegian about how he's just bought a bigger speedboat, or something. I found myself almost moved by the summer jollity of it all and how everything in the Norwegian summer seems specifically designed to create the perfect outdoor holiday lifestyle.

Later I was invited aboard Zoph's neighbour, the Bavaria 30 and we sat in the cockpit and cheered gently when there was a power cut that stopped the crooner in his tracks for a full half hour. Perhaps that was how the crooner made his money. Someone had paid to get him to shut up for a while. The visit to the Bavaria was an opportunity to see how the most deprived end of Norwegian society lives. Everyone in Norway has a boat, of course. Sailing yachts are apparently a lot cheaper than motor ones and the upper echelons drive dirty great gin palaces, the middle classes big motor cruisers or Hallberg Rassy 45 footers and the workers wee motor cruisers, smaller Hallbergs or 40ft Bavarias. This leaves the lowest rung of Norgian society and those people scraping along just – and only just – above the breadline. These poor unfortunates, who have somehow slipped through society's safety net, are reduced to driving about in Bavaria 30s. Yet somehow my hosts seemed to retain their self respect, however dire their circumstances, and were even able to offer me a crisp.

Once again I had realised that the forecast had changed a bit and that now the best window to get round Stad (Norway's most feared headland, you'll remember) was in two days time, when there would be gentle north-easterlies. The following three days were all to be strong south-westerlies, which was about as bad as it could get. The Molde diversion was therefore a bit of a pain as I motorsailed the 51 miles to Fosnavåg on the island of Bergsøya. I averaged nearly six knots all day motorsailing, mostly with the engine idling or on low revs, with the odd period under sail alone. A broad reach from Molde then turning onto a dead run to Ålesund, followed by a reach into open waters where the wind occasionally got up to twelve knots and gave us a good push.

In the afternoon I saw a Norwegian fishing boat called 'King's Cross' on the AIS. To a Norwegian this probably sounds like quite a posh, exalted name and not, as it must to all Brits, a train station. Most of the way I had a bit of favourable tide and by five thirty Zoph was rafted up in Fosnavåg on a big Norgian Najad.

Fosnavåg had been recommended as a gorgeous spot but was to my eyes a bit dull and lifeless. It was Saturday night but there were few people about except for in the one pub. A service centre for a small Island four miles across or so, it of course had three separate shopping centres with perhaps fifty shops. But only one pub with eight people in it. Still, at least the one pub was open on a Saturday night, even if I couldn't afford a beer in it.

There was one cruising boat smaller than Zoph. A 26ft Danish boat. I later realised however that this was the same Danish boat I had seen in Bessaker exactly four weeks before, with the drunken solo sailor. He had been heading south whilst I was heading north, so must have been going pretty slowly.

There was also a Swedish couple in a slim, lightweight, racy looking 35ft boat in the harbour and I established that they were heading for Stad the next day. I had a detailed forecast for Stad from Anna. The website www.yr.no, along with a million other things, gives a specific hour by hour detailed forecast for the waters off the peninsula, with graphs of wind strength and direction, wave height and direction and period. Wandering round harbours with this sort of forecast to impart makes you quite popular. Knowledge is power.

The Swedish woman suggested that we chum each other along the next day, for the security of it and because I had a chart plotter with AIS whilst they had only paper charts. The pilotage around Stad is not difficult but there is a lot of shipping and the possibility of fog. I'm glad she suggested it as they were on much the faster boat and I'd not like to have felt that I was forcing them to go slow. We agreed to leave at the pointlessly early time of 6.30 the next morning.

On the way up north I'd not been that worried by the Stad passage, but all the hushed awestruck tones with which the Norges discussed it had got to me a bit. The fog rolling in through the sounds to Måløy on the way up had been portentous. I had beaten Stad by rushing past just before it had unleashed its fury and it blew and pissed down on me too late, after I had already passed it. This time, perhaps, it was going to wreak revenge

As I dozed off for a few hours kip I reflected that on this trip, since Port Edgar, I'd done nearly fifty days solo sailing and that, If I pressed on and did the 65 miles to Florø tomorrow, it may well be my last solo passage of the trip. Anna was joining me in Florø at the end of the week, then I'd be looking for a crew to cross the North Sea again. "Not bad", I thought, "fifty days and 1800 miles solo and not an accident or serious incident of any sort. No major cock-ups or ramming pontoons. Nothing".

Ouch

The next morning I motored out of the harbour at five and a half knots and drove at full pelt straight into a dirty great rock, holing the boat and doing thousands of pounds worth of damage.

This was not a submerged and unmarked rock you understand. This rock was well above water and part of an entirely obvious man-made causeway which was itself marked by a twelve foot high, perfectly obvious lattice tower with a bloody great light on it. It was broad daylight and the visibility was about a mile. The rock, on the other hand was – well – 0 feet away.

I was following the Swedes down a narrow, well marked channel out to sea when I turned on the autopilot and went below briefly to check the computer for course and any shipping. When I emerged what seemed like only seconds later the starboard hand lattice tower was about a yard to port of the cockpit. Thinking 'this is it, we're going to hit', I banged the engine into full reverse and ripped the tiller pilot off the tiller. There was an immediate sickening crunch and the bow lifted. I don't think we were going that fast when we hit as I wasn't even thrown off my feet. I reversed off the rock and went below, expecting to see water gushing in, there was nothing. Back on deck I went to the bow and peered over. There seemed to be superficial damage to the starboard side and quite a bit gouged out of the point of the bow, just above the waterline. I removed the engine cover and looked in the bilge, there was no water getting in. The Swedes had seen that I had stopped and come back to investigate. My heart still thumping and hands shaking slightly I suggested we carry on. The Swedes concurred, though their expressions clearly registered the thought that they had thrown in their lot with an utter nutter.

An hour or two later, as we were approaching Stad (Norway's most... you get the picture), I had a wee pump of the bilge, which was full of water. Again I removed the engine cover and had a squint into the bilge, a steady trickle of water was getting in – no more than a pint a minute or so. I monitored this for a while and it didn't get any worse so again I decided to carry on. The hole must have been just above the waterline and leaking when we were moving forward but not when stopped.

After another while, as murky ships passed a mile away

Heading for Norway's most feared headland

in the half mile visibility, the Swedes asked if we should continue in the bad vis. It did look menacing: the low clouds looking like they might drop to sea level at any time, the piss-poor visibility and the grey disturbed sea surging in different direction. Buoyed up by the AIS, on which I could clearly see all the shipping and knew none of it was a threat, I persuaded them to carry on. As we were discussing this a fast hydrofoil ferry sped past at thirty knots. Its signal never appeared on the AIS at all. The bugger must have had it switched off. I didn't mention this to the Swedes so as not to worry them further.

Round Stad a ship appeared coming towards us. It seemed to be pitching a lot and crashing down big waves. 'Bloody hell' I thought 'there must be some waves over there'. But he was still pitching as he passed us . The six foot swell was with us and long enough to be comfortable, whereas for the fifty metre coaster battering into the waves at ten knots the wavelength was just exactly wrong.

I still think that 'Dangerous Waves' on the Norwegian charts just means 'Waves' and that the likes of the Pentland Firth and Corryvreckan could take Stad and Hustadvika in a fight with one hand tied behind their backs. Waves is waves however and apparently there's a plan to dig a tunnel, big enough to take large ships, through the Stad peninsula, so that no Norwegian shall ever have to put up with a wave. When I'd first heard about this plan, in early June, I'd thought it was a non-starter and a bit of a joke. Having seen just how much civil engineering has gone on to join up the bits of rural Norway I'm now quite surprised they've not dug it already.

Without further incident (well how many incidents do you want?) I arrived and tied up on the pontoon in Måløy, gathering a small crowd of amused motorboaters who all wanted the full humiliating story. Later we were joined by a forty foot sailing boat, which turned out to be the one with the French skipper that Zoph had rafted up on her first night in Bergen on June 1st. At that time I had decided that the skipper was probably gay. This time his wife and three kids suggested otherwise.

I had intended going on to Florø after checking the damage, but seeing that it looked worse from the pontoon than it did from the foredeck I decided I'd better not push it and to stay and at least give it a temporary repair.

The Swedes were nice about it and said that "it could happen to anyone" but I knew that it could only happen to an idiot and that they were thinking "what a moron". They suggested that there may have been a bit of cross-current taking us sideways before I hit the rock, but again I can't see how there can have been. One possibility is that, when I hit the autopilot button, it hadn't actually engaged and was still on standby. But the bottom line is that I shouldn't have gone below while we were still in the narrow channel. The time of day, anxiety about Stad and the insane sleepy half-belief that because Zoph was following another boat the autopilot would just sort of follow it are my poor excuses.

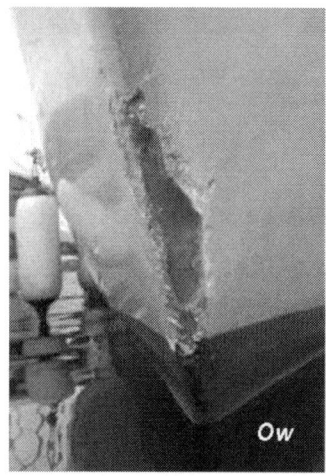
Ow

The Swedish yacht rounds Statt

...followed by a holed Zoph. (It's not as bad as it looks, honest)

That I had been sailing on my own for too long was amply demonstrated by the fact that, when I considered blaming the crash on a faulty autopilot I immediately felt that I couldn't because that would in some way be disloyal to the autopilot. For a long time I had been talking to bits of boat but now I had started investing human characteristics into all sorts of entirely inanimate objects.

Having rushed up and down Norway I had been wondering how I was going to counter my obsession with continuing to travel thirty to sixty miles every day when the time came to slow down. Rounding Stad meant I was near to my destination of Florø, where Anna was to join me, and it was time to slow down. Hitting a dirty great rock and holing the boat was a pretty effective way of slowing myself down.

Måløy is a Norwegian town of some two thousand people, so it has seven shipyards. Five of them are far too big to consider dealing with piddling little repairs to wee yachts and at the smallest one, on Monday morning, it was recommended that I try the second smallest one, which specialises in building and fixing fibreglass boats. As I Brompted the three miles over there in the pissing rain I had depressing visions of my reception. The sucking of air through teeth, the shaking of heads, the barely suppressed incredulity at my request to get anything done before at least October. "That's a winter job mate"… "We just can't get the staff"… "We might be able to do something for you in November"… "We don't do that sort of work because there's no demand for it"…

Arriving at the boatyard I said "I've got a small yacht and because I'm an idiot I rammed it into a rock, can you help?" "Sure, no problem" they said. "Bring the boat round and we'll take a look". I cycled back to Zoph and motored round to the boatyard, where I arrived at midday. By 3.15 in the afternoon Zoph was back in the water with the job done. She had been lifted in an eighty tonne travelling hoist, the damage above and below the waterline inspected, sanded off, dried out prepared, fibreglassed, dried again, painted and the boat put back in the water. The cost of the repair was about three hundred quid. On the downside, the cost of the lift in the hoist more usually used for large ferries was also three hundred quid. The last major job the yard did was building a hundred-passenger hydrofoil ferry for Shell's Flotta gas terminal in Orkney, so Zoph was just a wee speck in the huge lifting gear.

Zoph in a hoist designed for supertankers

During the whole process the entire smiling, contented workforce of the boatyard wandered around smoking and drinking coffee, offering me coffee and chatting. It was an entirely positive experience. When I came to pay the bill their apparatus wouldn't accept any of my cards. I said I'd go to a bank and get cash. "Yeah, whatever" said the boss "don't worry, tomorrow will be fine, there's no hurry. Leave the boat in our dock tonight if you want, you can stay there and plug into our electricity, whatever".

The only slight negative was that they didn't quite get the shape of Zoph's petite nose right. It looked like a bit of a wonky conk to me. They are professional, but more used to putting slap on old fishing boats than doing invisible mends on yachts. For that reason I opted for just a couple of coats of temporary paint rather than the full gel coat. It would need more work when I got home, but Zoph was fixed and watertight, albeit slightly scarred.

I thought the insurance company might be a stumbling block since, instead of getting two quotes and clearing it with them beforehand, I had the job done unilaterally then phoned them up to tell them. All I needed to do, however, was to explain the circumstances and the dangers of leaving a leaky boat afloat in 45 knot winds and they immediately agreed to pay. Later, back in Edinburgh, the startling speed and efficiency with which they agreed to pay for the rather expensive extra work was quite exemplary. I'm not one for waxing lyrical about insurance companies but can heartily recommend 'Nautical Insurance Services'.

During the process of getting Zoph fixed I cycled into town to fetch dosh. In the guest harbour the wee Danish boat was on the pontoon and I spoke to the previously pissed skipper and his monosyllabic, elderly companion. He'd managed only three hundred miles since I first bumped into him in Bessaker exactly a month before. Apparently he'd also hit a rock (in more forgivable circumstances, due to engine failure) and had to call out the lifeboat. He then spent twenty two days in one village trying to get the damage fixed. He appeared to be just exactly as pissed as during our first encounter and I wondered if he was, in fact, not temporarily pissed but permanently a bit spaced out due to drugs or a medical condition.

The following morning was virtually windless at deck level in the perfect shelter of the Måløy Verft dock. The anemometer – which was going through one of its more lucid patches and was working, registered up to 45 knots at the top of the mast. I registered pissing down and soaking wet in the cockpit. Under the circumstances I thought I'd stay put for a bit, to which the boatyard folk were amenable.

In the afternoon the wind abated a bit and they wanted me shifted to get a ship in the hoist. I thought it was about time I left anyway and motored off into a force six, gusting seven. Before I'd left the bay the GPS registered two thousand miles travelled since Port Ed. I turned so that the wind was behind me and motored the short distance to the pleasantly scruffy little visitors' pontoon at Rugsund, perfectly sheltered behind lush trees.

As I made to round the fully occupied pontoons and see if there was any space the other side, folk on converted fishing boats started gesticulating wildly that I shouldn't. I rafted up on one of the old wooden fishing boats. It seems that the morning's winds had put undue strain on the knackered and wobbly old pontoon - which had a load of over a hundred tonnes in the form of visiting big old ships – and it had started wandering downwind across the bay. The windward side was now a cat's cradle of hundred metre long lines desperately strung between the fishing boats or the pontoon and every available rock and tree on the other side of the bay.

Most of the boats in Rugsund were travelling together and heading for a traditional boat festival at Fosnavåg, where I'd hit a major rock two days before. They were stuck south of Stad with continuing strong winds, albeit blowing in the right direction for them. The boats didn't look all that traditional to me. There were, as I've mentioned, a few wooden fishing boats used as yachts and what you'd definitely describe as a ship. A cross between a ferry and a gentleman's yacht, about a hundred feet long and built, apparently in the south of England in the 1970s.

Later, a yacht with a red ensign hove into view – a Scandinavian looking Scanyacht 39 - and rafted up on another pile of fishing boats. I chatted to the skipper in the pouring rain. He runs RYA courses, mostly for Brits, in Norway. So if you fancy doing your Yachtmaster Tidal somewhere where there's no tides, no passage planning, fickle winds you can't sail in and a marina every mile, he's your man. It'd be a doddle.

While we were chatting a rotund moustachioed gent from the traditional boat crew invited us into the big barn of a building next to the dock to eat crab, drink beer (B.Y.O.) and, ominously, sing songs. In the barn about a

In places the sea really was this colour

hundred absurdly jolly Norgians were ranged either side of a set of long tables. Several spokesmen got to their feet to welcome us and press crab meat upon us (which I'm afraid I had to refuse, having just developed a serious allergy to seafood the previous year – what a bugger). They sat us down and questioned us. Pretty soon the dreaded singing started. Many copies of a ring-bound book bearing the title 'Sommer 2008' were passed round. They actually print an annual songbook for their jolly campfire get-togethers. The fifty page book was packed full of dreadful old standards, including, inevitably, several in English which they tried to force us to sing. I managed to croak out a few words of 'The Wild Rover' and by now most people were too drunk to tell if it was in tune.

Then a hush was called for and the speeches started. The interminable speeches in which various of the leaders thanked everyone for being great and everyone clapped and laughed at each sentence and said how great the leading folk were. Then they wheeled out the barn's owner, who gave us at least an hour about its history, all in Norwegian of course. He had prepared a PowerPoint presentation and at the beginning he unfolded a small laptop and set it on a low table in one corner of the massive barn. I was sat more or less in the opposite corner about thirty yards away. We were all expected to follow his presentation while staring at this pin-prick of light, which occasionally changed colour subtly as he flicked through the slides. No-one seemed to find this presentation style odd and they hung on his every word, waking me an hour or so later with their rapturous applause.

The barn was a reconstruction of an old trading post. The reconstruction had been destroyed and rebuilt again ten years ago. Yet to Norwegians this was still a very old building. In Britain we have a very precious approach to history. We keep ancient monuments exactly as they are, preserving in aspic their crumbling battlements. It would be unthinkable actually to fix them. With wooden buildings Norwegians take a more pragmatic view. They need maintenance and maintenance includes replacing parts and sometimes whole buildings. In the World Heritage Site in Bergen consisting of the old buildings along the dock, one of the ancient listed buildings was in the middle of being built, from scratch, when I was last there.

After the speeches there was more sing-song, much of which I escaped by trying to find phone reception in the pissing rain up a small hill. When I returned the sprogs were under the spotlight as about seven kids aged between eight and twelve sang a prepared song whilst the adults sat rapt with beatific smiles. They sang a modern English language pop song which, rather disturbingly, exhorted their baby to sex them up. The parents seemed to find this perfectly in order and at the end the applause was deafening.

I left soon after, reflecting that the main characteristic of the evening had been a total, utter lack of cynicism amongst the Norwegians. The whole thing reminded me a bit of New Zealand, but mostly of the sort of event that might have taken place in the Shire and been written about by Tolkien. Overgrown hobbits all having fun and nobody saying anyone's singing was crap or disagreeing with the speakers.

It was still blowy the following morning but had gone down to a force five south westerly as I cast off and motored the sixteen miles to Kalvåg. This was the first time since Anstruther that I had just battered against the wind and waves under engine all day, but with the long fetch up Froysjoen facing south west and the open sea there was little choice. A bit bouncy but perfectly easy. Battering along I did think how lucky I had been with the wind direction so far. Various proper traditional boats passed me going the other way. Apparently there was to be a massed gathering south of Stad then a huge convoy would attempt to go round it the following morning with a lifeboat leading them. Wimps.

Kalvåg, on Frøya Island, was a nice, scrubbed, tasteful village which gave the impression of being a very controlled re-development in a traditional style. A bit less scruffily organic than most places in Norway. I got a space on a huge wide 'L'-shaped pontoon and bought belated birthday presents for Anna from a arty-farty shop run by an Irish woman. There was a scruffy motorboat in the harbour flying a Shetland flag and with the legend 'Muckle Flugga Charters' emblazoned on the side. I did establish however that they'd not chartered it to cross the North Sea but were the owners of the charter operation on their holidays.

The rest of the day was distinguished only by my almost irresistible desire to murder the couple of twelve year old sprogs who razzed round and round the harbour in inflatables with outboards until 11.30 at night. Surely the noise and the wash must have been annoying their parents as well and they also had to pay for the petrol. This is standard Norwegian behaviour and I can't really see why the parents don't just tell the sprogs that if they want to play in the dinghy they should use the bloody oars. Oooo I was quite grumpy about it, I can tell you.

The following day I had a wee sail south but the breeze was fluky and the

Kalvag

motor soon on as I investigated a couple of astonishingly sheltered wee harbours down intricate channels on the island of Fanøya. As I gently drifted into one little harbour and was turning round in the tiny tight space to leave again I was hailed by a woman on the pier. "Are you from Shetland" she said. I explained that what she was looking at was a St Andrew's flag and that the Shetland flag, though the same colours, has vertical white stripes offset a little from the centre. She seemed disappointed. Several people I met in Norway could identify the Shetland flag but not the Scottish one and the few Shetland boats I saw there all seem to fly their flag instead of the red ensign. It is testament to the obvious connections between Norway and Shetland that these wee islands are more recognisable than the country of which they are purportedly part.

Then it was on to Florø. This had been my destination for exactly three weeks since the north end of Lofoten. All that time I'd had Florø guest harbour as the waypoint on the GPS and as I reached it – or at least within about ten metres of it – I'd done 636 miles southwards in nineteen days plus two days off. Despite the set-backs of the previous few days there was some pleasure in this arrival, which did seem almost like a homecoming.

In Florø I filled up with diesel – the first time since Lofoten. I'd used 118.61 litres in 82 engine hours. That's 1.45 litres an hour whilst motoring. I know a sailing boat should be able to do it with no fuel, but that's really not bad for cruising in sheltered waters. I'm sure the passage from Molde, the one round Statt and the batter to windward the day before had latterly made the figure look worse.

Floro Marina

On Holiday

All I had to do now was wait for Anna to arrive for her annual holiday. Now you may well be thinking "Holiday! What does he need a holiday for? He's been on holiday for over two months" and you'd have a point. But I'd sailed for fifty six days sailing and 2050 miles from Port Edgar. In my self-indulgent world, the fact that I no longer had to put in long passages every day and had over a month to go the remaining 200 miles or so to Stavanger felt like a much needed break. In effect a holiday from my extended holiday.

For only the second time since Lerwick, 50 days before, I didn't go anywhere the next day. I stayed put in the guest harbour in Florø, which was packed with the usual motorised gin palaces and, for once, quite a number of cruising sailing boats. In particular there were a lot of Swedish boats, mostly forty to fifty foot Najads and one-off ketches with ungainly poop decks like pirate ships. There was one 35 footer looking tiny by comparison, but as usual Zoph was by far the smallest foreigner.

Having passed south of Stad I was now back in the land of the 'sternshroom' and these were much in evidence amongst the motor boats. Further north folk practice conventional anchoring if they are to anchor at all. Most people wouldn't dream of anchoring and insist on a pontoon with electricity every night. Most boats in the north are however fitted with a bow anchor of some sort. South of Stad, where the tides are no more than a metre, nobody would dream of dropping an anchor from the bow and most of the motor boats are fitted only with a stern anchor.

With a keen eye for fashionable sleekness these are often designed more to complement the moulded lines of the plastic stern than actually to stick to the bottom of the sea. The most popular design seems to be a gleaming, perfectly round stainless steel mushroom – the sternshroom. This is casually tossed off the back of the boat on the end of about 5 metres of woven cloth tape. The bow is driven onto the shore and tied to a tree, a rock, or one of the millions of mooring rings and 'T's driven into the rocks around a million perfect anchorages. I doubt whether these sternshrooms would hold if there was ever a breeze or – worse still – a ripple through the anchorage, but this seems not to worry the massed ranks of barbecuing speedsters.

Florø was a pleasant wee town. It has the usual couple of thousand people with about as many shipyards and as much industry as the Clyde had fifty years ago and more infrastructure than any town in Scotland. The public swimming pool, for example, is a huge new modernist building jutting out over a blue sea with fabulous views of the mountains to the south. All winter the Norgians can flop about in deck chairs around their heated glass-boxed infinity pool, gazing at picture-postcard snow-capped peaks. Being a town of a couple of thousand inhabitants, of course, it has at least four marinas, each for two or three hundred boats.

After a day spent in Florø frantically scrubbing and cleaning out the detritus of a couple of months slovenly living, I took the fast ferry the next day to Bergen to meet Anna. On the one hand it was mildly depressing to take three hours at thirty knots for the journey which took Zoph a couple of days. On the other hand it was quite refreshing to sit and doze in comfort in first-class aeroplane seats, leaving the navigation to someone else. We sped down the narrow channels and by-ways, stopping for what seemed like an instant at various jetties to pick up passengers. Again I was struck by how well the Norgians use the sea as an essential transport link – something that we in Britain gave up doing a century or more ago.

Strolling along the quay in Bergen I saw a few old acquaintances I'd made in various far-flung places. A Swedish yacht I'd seen in Bud, Radsund and Molde. The scruffy old Shetland motorboat who's owner I had chatted to in Gremista marina in Lerwick. The mad Danish bloke from Bodø in his wee 26 footer, who I'd seen – and marvelled at the mental state of – in Bessaker, Fosnavåg and Måløy. He was still just as mad and wittering on about how he couldn't make his computer work. I usually give people the benefit of

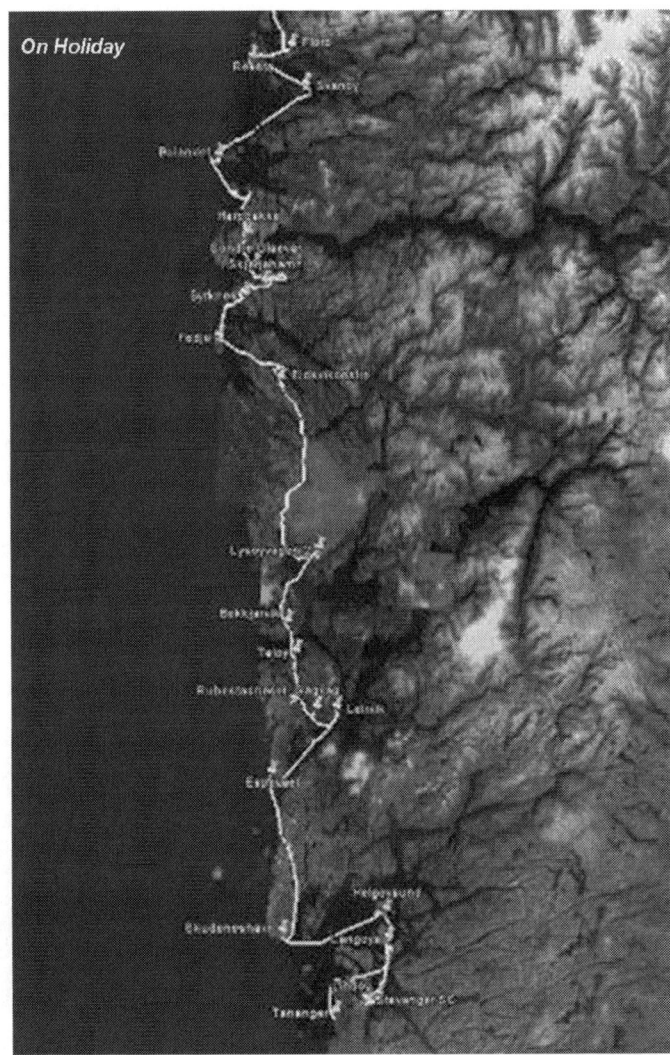

On Holiday

the doubt when it comes to computers and assume they know more than me. In his case I suspect he hadn't plugged it in.

Wandering Zophless amongst the boats I felt somewhat emasculated. I stopped to offer help with lines to one yacht, but I was no longer a trustworthy seafarer, just a tourist in civvies – one of the milling throng – and the yachties refused my amateur help in a rather snotty way.

Anna arrived and managed to make it into the centre of Bergen from the airport, despite the fact that the buses stop running – for some odd reason - on Saturdays only, at 5.30 pm. Every other day, including Sundays, they run well into the night. We went out for a meal to celebrate her recent birthday and despite vowing not to spare any expense, ended up with the inevitable damp and disappointing pizza and a glass of beer for about sixty quid. There probably are fine haut cuisine opportunities to be had in Norway, but you've really got to think forty quid a course and fifty quid for a bottle of wine before the kitchen gets in the least high.

The next day we did the tourist thing round Bergen, including walking up to the viewpoint at Floyen – over 1000ft above the city. On my last visit Fiona, Ian and I had taken the wimp's way up on the funicular railway. Anna and I weren't feeling particularly intrepid, but on a July weekend it was less hassle to walk up the mountain than queue for the railway.

In the afternoon we had another fast razz by hydrofoil back up the highways and byways north of Bergen. The only really memorable bit was when we spotted another traditional open Norwegian sailing boat. I'd seen a few of these double-ended Viking style boats, but this one was particularly memorable on two counts. It was being towed fast by a large fishing boat and it was almost entirely under water. Clearly it had been towed too fast and become swamped. Now the stern was wholly under water and if the towing ship had stopped it would have sunk. As it was it was only kept barely afloat by sort of semi-surfing. We could only imagine that they would have to seek out an area of shallow beaches – rare in these parts – to try and ground her. We sped past in an instant and were back on Zoph by the evening.

I was concerned to make Anna's time on Zoph a proper holiday and not an oilskin-clad Arctic Ocean ordeal, so didn't want to head off into any nasty weather the next day. We had plenty of time anyway. That's why I had rushed southwards – so that now we could take our time and pick

Feed the birds. A sprog being eaten by seagulls in Bergen

Reksta

the good weather for travelling. There was a gale warning in force for the waters around Florø, but it had never arrived, was due to subside by lunchtime anyway and the weather was hot and sunny. So we decided to head off in the afternoon and hoisted full sail in a gentle ten knot northerly breeze, heading out through the narrow rock-strewn channels to

Svanoy

the west of Florø. A very pleasant day, though I suspected we wouldn't really have enough wind to sail properly.

Within twenty minutes we were reduced to deep reefed main and staysail as the northerly blew force six gusting seven and a short splashy chop sent breakers over the rocks all around us. With meticulous planning I hadn't bothered to look at the charts and familiarise myself with the intricate channels. Anna was therefore dispatched to consult the laptop chartplotter, which, with a single flourish, she immediately managed to shut down. The process of rebooting the bloody thing – including locating and plugging in the miniscule 'dongle' that enables the charts – takes about ten minutes. When you are rushing blind between the breakers down unknown channels in a force seven, swearing at someone, this seems more like an hour.

Anyway, to cut a long story long, we managed to get the charts back and decided to head for the nearest island port, Rognaldsvågen on Reksta, which we did at over six knots under double reefed main only. We squeezed through the guarding rocks on a lee shore into the harbour, which turned out to be uncomfortably exposed to the north. We tied to the substantial new wooden pier however and Anna refused to countenance nipping out past the rocks and round to the south of the island, where there was perfect shelter in a harbour three miles away by sea and a hundred yards by land. So we sat that night tied to wooden piles by a cat's cradle of ropes as Zoph pitched around as if she were well out to sea. It was like sleeping on a sort of ocean crossing simulator. Tied to the land but with the motion of the ocean.

It was an inauspicious start, but the sun was out, the walks ashore scenic and the mooring safe enough. We were on proper holiday and slept well in our soothing rocking cradle.

After this experience of heading out to the outer islands, we decided to head inland for more shelter. The conditions were light in the morning but due to get both wet and windy later. We had a nice gentle reach under full sail at four knots, followed by a fast reach at six knots as the wind increased and took us

round Askrova island and into a sheltered bay on Svanøy. Here the pontoons were busy, mostly with the partying ships I had seen a few days earlier in Rugsund. Being wee has its advantages however and Zoph was able to squeeze into a creek on the island side of the pontoons and berth in a perfectly sheltered narrow cut in shallower water.

Later a small German steel yacht rafted up on us. Though longer than Zoph at nine metres, this wee boat looked considerably smaller, with about a foot of freeboard aft and a low cabin top. One of the very few cruising boats I met in over two months which was, arguably at least, smaller than Zoph. Gratifyingly, its skipper pointed at Zoph's garishly painted windvane with its shamelessly copied pictures and asked whether I was an artist.

A board for tourists advertised a marked walk to the other side of the island, which we duly took. This mostly rough and boggy path had been marked within the last few days with obsessive amounts of barely dry blue paint adorning every tree, rock and tussock for miles. Two thirds of the way round there was a metal box with, inevitably, a visitors' book and pen. Everyone who walked up the track was expected to leave effusive comments about the fantastic quality of the experience. Those Norgians really know how to organise a rural leisure pursuit.

On the way back we got to stroke inquisitive deer. Something which Anna regretted on finding later that her legs were peppered with ticks, which needed prizing out. I'm told that being sucked at by ticks in the West of Scotland can leave you with Lyme disease, a condition in which you are rendered lethargic and useless for years. The jury's still out on whether Anna has this condition. After all she exhibited most of the symptoms before encountering the ticks.

On the way back we saw a sign for a craft shop which broke the current Norwegian record for its poor opening hours. Apparently it opens for one hour every Sunday in July and at no other time. They pay the rent on the shop to open it for four hours a year.

Back on Zoph, sheltering from the gathering dreich, we were approached by a rather hippy young French yachtsman who had just arrived with his wife and about 4 sprogs – all under eight years old – more or less directly from France. Pointing at Zoph's gaudily painted wind vane he said, in a suitably romantic French accent "Zat is ze most beautiful wind vane I have ever seen". Zoph and I blushed.

The next morning, as we motored away from the pontoon, he and his wife stood arm in arm, grinning wistfully at us and waving us goodbye like people out of a David Lynch film. These real adventurers seemed to have decided that us holidaymakers were more impressive and intrepid than we really were – or felt.

We reached in a fickle wind at between three and six knots all day the twenty four miles out west to the island outpost of Bulandet. A couple of times the engine went on and the jib was furled for a while, but after Stavenes, in open water exposed to the north we were under full sail all the way. The small chop created by the south west wind acted against the two metre swell from the north to create a slightly menacing sea, which wasn't helped by the slate-grey sky and dull conditions as we sailed round the apparently famous island of Alden, known as Den Norske Hesten – the Norse Horse.

Bulandet is a collection of islands on Norway's western extremity supposed to contain its most westerly permanently inhabited settlement. It has a reputation for great beauty and tweeness, hence our visit. Rafting up in the busy new concrete fishing harbour against a Bavaria we were a little disappointed in this apparent paradise. There was nothing really wrong with it but practically every harbour I'd seen in Norway had been better looking.

We braved the midges to walk around the islands. This was nowhere near as life threatening as a west of Scotland midge experience, but mildly annoying nonetheless. Bulandet is a series of small islands, most within a few yards of one another and linked by short bridges. Within half an hour we'd bagged about five more islands. Away from the harbour the scenery improved and the multitude of little natural harbours opened up in the gathering darkness.

We continued wandering through the tweenery. At the western end of the

The skies clear on Bulandet

Bulandet

islands is a small hill and a path advertising a viewpoint. Much against her will I dragged Anna up the hill to peer at the view through the gloom.

And then it happened. As we stared at the vista of a thousand low islands stretching to infinity a line of blue sky appeared in the west and quickly swept the cloud away. The low sun shone on one of the most fantastic views either of us has ever seen. The shallow bays between the convoluted islands were lit up in cobalt blue like coral lagoons. Every little island had a collection of improbably cute painted wooden houses. Had hobbits been seafaring creatures, this would have been their harbour. The fantastic light and stillness of the scene left us quite breathless.

Bulandet panorama

Summer

And it didn't end there. From that moment on, for the next week we didn't see a single cloud. For the week after that the weather conspired to be sunny all day with, on two or three occasions a shower. But the rain always came after eleven p.m. leaving the days unremittingly sunny and tropical. For the whole of the next fortnight we had hot, almost tropical conditions of the sort that had me leaping into the sea after breakfast just to cool off a bit. And this pseudo Mediterranean fortnight was so much more enjoyable than if it had actually taken place in the Med. Practically every night we had our pick of gorgeous, perfectly sheltered and deserted anchorages to swan about in, with perfectly clean seas to swim in. It was a fortnight neither of us will forget in a hurry.

The first day of this fortnight saw us motoring across a glassy sea to Sandøy – the island just west of Bulandet – through some of the narrowest and most convoluted channels I'd seen so far. A downside of the perfect weather was, of course, no actual sailing, but in this sun we weren't complaining. We then headed for Hardbakke via two or three anchorages mentioned in our Norwegian language pilot. The first was billed as a 'busy and popular harbour' and was utterly deserted with, unusually, not even any rings in the rocks to tie to. The second was supposed to be 'an undiscovered pearl' and was utterly mobbed. A bay filled with pontoons, the boats were rafted up so deep that I think this harbour might have been the only genuinely full harbour I saw in Norway. This pearl had definitely been discovered.

Though Hardbakke was quite busy we managed to get a large chunk of guest quay to ourselves, discovering later that this was perhaps because the Dutch bloke who patrolled the quay and acted as Harbourmaster, wanted an outrageous fifty Norks (that's Norwegian Kroner of course) for the use of electricity.

The next day we had another gentle motor in the sun via a some more perfect anchorages, to moor fore and aft to a rock near a pair of partying

motorboats. A couple of swims in the 20° sea and a trouncing of Anna at scrabble rounded off yet another almost boringly perfect day.

We went on to the popular weekend town of Eivindvik the next day, where we tied to a pontoon and had a showers in the run-down facilities. Eivindvik was severely marred by some of the most extreme rudeness I came across in Norway. Everybody seemed a little shirty and unhelpful, but the woman in the hotel who I tried to buy an ice cream from was spectacularly rude. Perhaps after two days of tropical summer the heat was getting to everyone.

We didn't fancy staying so motored on to the supposedly quiet anchorage of Skjerjehamn. This was

Down some of the narrowest channels so far

billed as an undeveloped, deserted anchorage, but having just seen someone wearing a tee shirt featuring Skjerjehamn as a party town I wasn't sure it was going to be so quiet.

The new complex of pontoons had about a hundred boats of all kinds rafted up on them. They'd all showed up for a concert of Beatles favourites being given by an apparently famous young duo in the swanky, brand new restaurant and concert hall. The pontoons weren't built in a terribly good place and were subject to quite a bit of wash from passing speedboats. I suspect that they would be untenable in any sort of strong westerly or north-westerly conditions.

The place was hooching with partying Bergenites and the holiday atmosphere was palpable. Where else but in Norway would five hundred people show up for an evening gig in speedboats and a swim in the bay before going straight into the concert in swimming gear at sunset at eleven pm?

I don't really know why people pay money (in this case twenty five quid) for these summer gigs, since you can inevitably hear the music perfectly well – indeed a little too well - from your boat on the pontoon. One reason, I suppose, might be to avoid the midges, which were of almost west-coast intensity here and did their best to spoil things.

Before the concert I was hailed enthusiastically from the dock by a wee round man. It took me a while to recognise him I must confess, but I finally placed him to the motorboat I'd been next to on the pontoon in Henningsvær, some eight hundred miles earlier. I'd also seen him in Halsa, near the Svartisen Glacier. He was from Tromsø and a long way from home.

It's rare to find the standard Norwegian motorboat a significant distance from home. I'd often thought about Zoph's tortoise-and-hare paradox as I'd been passed by innumerable speeding gin palaces over the last two months. The gin palaces were invariably tearing along at twenty five knots and their crews probably largely contemptuous of Zoph's crawling four or five knot pace. But they only went at twenty five knots for an hour or two. Scarcely any of them went more than a hundred miles or so from home. Apart from anything else they couldn't afford the fuel. Depending on their size and speed they consumed between twenty and a hundred litres an hour. Zoph, if we need to motor, uses about one and a half and the seven hundred miles from Lofoten to Florø was done on less than a tank.

They might sneer at our speed, but the gin palace occupants were invariably impressed at the distance we'd come. To most, Scotland was a distant foreign country of legend. In the end the tortoise out-does the hare every time. With the odd exception, such as my wee chum from Tromsø.

We broke the record for narrow and tortuous channels the next day as we motored between islands over what the chartplotter swore was land and under what it promised were ten metre high cables. But locals had told us it was possible and so it proved. We nipped into the idyllic harbour round the back of Birkenes to take a look. If anything places were getting even more painfully twee.

We dropped anchor for lunch inside the island of Kjelling. After a swim I let out a fishing line and was surprised to pull up two pollock in quick succession. That's was dinner sorted, though Anna was not terribly keen on fish thrashing about in the cockpit in their death throes.

After lunch we actually managed a sail. A reach at three to four knots to the island of Fedje, home of Bergen port control. This is yet another island with a ludicrously sheltered harbour that it's difficult to believe is natural. How many islands are there in Norway with a neat round hole in the middle and a narrow channel out to sea? What are that chances of that happening in even one island without the design intervention of someone like Slartibartfast?

Being wee we managed to bag a finger pontoon space whilst most of the other sailing boats had to raft up rather dodgily outside the pontoons. The other two British boats in Fedje – the first I'd seen for a while – were a dive boat from Oban and the 'Thermopylae Clipper' – one of the clipper round the world yachts on a delivery trip to join the tall ships race in Måløy. Neither of these would fit on the pontoons at all and had to tie up round on the fish quay.

Fedje had a potentially brilliant innovation for hopping across the harbour and avoiding the mile walk around to the shop. A self-propelled chain ferry. The idea was you all piled onto a floating steel platform while one volunteer – or mug – wound the wheel to propel you across. There were several problems with this set up. Firstly, by the time you were at the other side of the thirty metre wide channel the volunteer was so knackered he wasn't up to walking the fifty yards to the shop. Secondly, the shore-based mechanisms

for recovering the ferry didn't work, So you only had a fifty-fifty chance of being able to use it, since it had to be on the same side as you to start with. If it were busy this wouldn't be a problem, but on a sleepy Norgian island you could be waiting for days.

Boringly enough, we had more of the same motoring in tropical conditions over glassy smooth sea the next day. We anchored for a swim and lunch at the head of a wee Fjord called Hola on Fosnøy, then pootled on into the almost landlocked waters of Lindes through the odd, canalised Lindes Slusene. This was a five metre wide channel with brick walls either side through which the current flows at up to five knots. I didn't read about this bit in the pilot until we'd already gone through it once. Fortunately we had the tide with us on the way out and it was nowhere near five knots, but in a land with few tides five knots in a five metre wide channel is the nautical equivalent of the Cresta Run. It is of course complicated by the tendency of Norwegian speedboats to razz through it at twenty knots without bothering to wait and see if there's anything coming the other way.

Anyway, we survived and pottered across to the narrow, heavily wooded Radsund. This was a weekend playground with yet a different atmosphere. Wooden 'huts' lined the steep sided, forested slopes tumbling down to narrow sounds which looked for all the world like inland rivers. In reality these 'huts' ranged from 'A' framed chalets to sprawling bungaloid mansions with their own pontoons. We seemed to be far away from the sea as river boats and speed boats motored between weekend retreats. The fast hydrofoil from Bergen zooming up the alleyways was one reminder that this was still the sea.

After poking into a few blind alleys and getting a bit lost we tied to a rock in a perfect, hurricane-proof anchorage, Eidsvik Oestre, which we had all to ourselves. From here we could see no sign of civilisation, despite the constant dim sound of internal combustion engines as wee boats plied out if sight amongst the many channels. We seemed to be the only people in Norway who actually rowed a tender and we drew odd looks from passing motorers as we took our evening rowing constitutional and watched the sun go down.

The seclusion of our anchorages was leading me into some grotesque practices. Notably skinny-dipping before breakfast. I was trying to develop a technique for catching fish by stunning them with the appalling sight. Afterwards we motored down the Radsund in the hot sun as slowly as possible to catch the tide through the narrows at the end. An apparent contradiction between the two pilot

Fedje

books over which direction the ebb and flow actually goes in turned out not to be. Somehow the tide seemed to flow one way down most of Radsund (against us) but the other way at the fast narrows at the same time. How it manages this is a mystery.

Both pilots are limited in their detail of tides and the like. The new Imray one typically says of everywhere "the tide

Eidsvik Oestre

flows north on the flood, south on the ebb, changing at half tide". Well if it changes at half tide, which blinkin' half is flowing in which bleedin' direction? I never did suss this out to my full satisfaction.

We motored past Bergen and into the anchorage at Smivagen on Tyssøy where I'd last been on June the second with Ian and Fiona. Now, in July, it was hooching with motor boats and sprogs plummeting into the sea off rocks, but we managed to squeeze into a wee space. As predicted, it being a Tuesday and therefore a school night, almost all the boats disappeared back off to Bergen and elsewhere by about eleven in the evening. Smivagen was left with us and two families out of small day boats who pitched their tents on the shore.

The weather remained tropical and demanded swimming, but some entertaining thunder and lightning that night had me removing the VHF aerial from the radio and the AIS aerial from the computer. Probably a futile gesture but I had visions of fried laptops.

Anna's rowing Masterclass in Eidsvik Oestre

The next morning we had some actual wind and beat south at four to five knots, bearing away onto a reach then slowing to a dead run into Lysøyvagen. Again a place I'd visited in early June and the site of my first swim of the season. We anchored for lunch and wandered off to look at the famed house of the famed violinist Ole Bull. He apparently resisted the temptation to be a Spanish toreador, despite his name. His over the top wedding cake house was a little laughable alongside the rest of Norway's sensible, but nonetheless twee architecture.

Though we left in the afternoon a combination of dodgy alternative anchorages and a minor domestic saw us return and tie up to a tree for the night. All of which gave Lysøyvagen the record as the most anchored in Zoph anchorage, with three stops. That night we had the first rain shower for seven days, but it had the decency to fall overnight when we didn't care, and the weather cleared nicely for the morning.

The next day dawned as hot and sunny as ever and we motored in the calm to the little town of Bekkjarvik. This had some nicely sheltered wooden quays right in the centre, but they were hooching with boats – mostly motorboats. We hung around for a bit however and got a good space against the quay when somebody left.

Bekkjarvik was a one horse, four shop town with, that day at least, a good holiday atmosphere. It's very much on the weekend route from Bergen for speedboaters who don't want to use too much fuel going too far afield. As usual, being an odd, small, foreign boat, people were reluctant to raft up on us until there was really no alternative, but later on we did get an old double-ended motor boat outside us.

As we sat in the sun in the afternoon we were hailed by a passing bus driver. Later he abandoned his bus and came to talk to me. He was an English bloke who had moved to Norway and seemed to be mildly insane. He wanted to sell his house and seemed to want me to buy it. Not only that, but he was apparently prepared just to swap it for our house. The fact that our house is in Edinburgh and he was from Watford or somewhere didn't seem to be an issue. I smiled and nodded politely and backed away slowly.

Since Bekkjarvik had four shops, one of them was of course a chandler better than practically any in Scotland. With their help I wired up the twelve volt fridge so that I could run it on shore power. In this weather the fridge was becoming as essential a piece of kit as the chart plotter.

More significantly, I checked my work email. I had decided that it was becoming untenable working for my then employer – for whom I'd worked for a quarter of a century. At the time I was on an unpaid sabbatical but regime changes and 'new-broom-syndrome' were making things difficult and I'd decided just to resign and leave with nothing. As I was about to resign however they announced a scheme of voluntary redundancies and early retirement. In Bekkjarvik I received an email saying that I had been accepted for this. So I had a choice – leave with nothing, or leave with a lump sum and nine years extra enhanced pension. Hmmm... what was I to do? Leave with no money or leave with money... Hmmm... As you can imagine I was in an agony of indecision for upwards of a millisecond. Celebrations ensued.

This was a major life-changing event, but the next day offered, in very a small way, one of the most surreal events I've ever experienced and one which made it feel nice to be part of the human race.

Once again it was a gentle motor in full sun the short distance to the anchorages at Teløy, near Fitjar. The island of Teløy is nearly cut in two by a series of lagoons with shallow bars across the entrance. We motored into the first, perfectly sheltered bay to find a couple of boats at anchor. We crossed the two metre bar into the second bay, where a couple of motor boats were tied to trees. We crossed the one and a half metre bar in the narrow channel to the third and innermost bay. We had this hundred metre diameter round bay entirely to ourselves and anchored in six metres in the middle. It is impossible to conceive of a better or more sheltered anchorage anywhere in the world. It is impossible to imagine what sort of weather could present a problem in this most perfect of anchorages.

Lysoyvagen

Tyssoy

Though there were boats moored in different place around Teløy and its neighbouring islands, there was such a super-abundance of anchorages that no-one came into our perfect bay. We spent the rest of the day swimming and sunbathing. I had discovered that the best place to sunbathe, given Zoph's narrow decks and lack of flat space, was lying on the overturned inflatable dinghy floating astern. On this day however it was too hot to lie for long and I kept having to flop into the sea to cool off. Things just couldn't get any better.

We wondered about the possibility of staying put for another few days instead of moving on. The only problem with these secluded anchorages, with no shops - or indeed any human habitation - for miles around, was getting fresh food. Fish was of course freely available, but nice fresh bread, for example, was becoming scarce. We wouldn't starve, but a stay in our splendid isolation would be marred by the lack of such provisions.

Anna was awoken the next morning at about 8.30 by the familiar mosquito buzz of a small outboard as a wee speedboat approached our private anchorage. The noise got closer and closer. There was a lull in the engine noise, a gentle THUMP as something hit Zoph, then the motor speeded up again and receded off into the distance. Curious and a little concerned I got up to inspect the damage – after half an hour more kip – and looked in the cockpit.

There was a plastic bag containing four fresh bread rolls. Things had got better. It seemed that every morning the local shop, about 5 miles away as the crow flies, dispatches a lad in a speedboat with a pile of bags of rolls. He whizzes down the tortuous channels to every anchorage within a five mile radius and makes a present of four bread rolls to every boat. The only economic point to this can be that the rolls come in a bag advertising the shop and you get a couple of tourist brochures. But there's no obligation to go to the shop, which was over an hour's motoring away. Anyway, we now had no need of a shop, since we had our breakfast rolls.

This quite surreal act had me briefly wondering whether we should just stay there forever. We had a free anchorage, fish to be had in the loch and free bread every day. I couldn't decide whether loaves and fishes or manna from heaven was the better biblical metaphor. Anna snapped me out of my mad reverie and we prepared to leave.

The weather had also come out of its reverie and we had cloud and actual rain for a bit as we motored, then beat under jib, being too lazy to raise the main. The rain stopped and the sky cleared as we motor-sailed to Rubbestadneset, (which means 'rubber band nest'), then on to reputedly lovely Sagvåg, which was not. Though a good sheltered harbour Sagvåg looked a bit

Teloy, land of loaves and fishes

depressed and worn out, as the name perhaps suggests, so we sailed round on a nice reach to the more major industrial town of Lærvik. The pontoons here are a little exposed to wash and the town nothing to write home about. But perhaps we were getting spoilt by the astonishing aesthetics of most places in Norway. In truth Lærvik was a perfectly reasonable town as nice as its Shetland near-namesake..

An excess of tweenery awaited us the following day as we headed to the outlying Atlantic islands of Espevær. There was bugger-all wind so we motored via a couple of harbours. The first was Mosterhamn, which had been our first real harbour on heading south from Bergen the previous year. I remembered it is fantastically twee, very small and perfectly sheltered. Now it looked very nondescript, quite open and exposed. This confirmed just how used we had become to the perfect little harbours of Norway. It must come as quite a shock to Norwegians, arriving in Scottish 'anchorages' and reading in the pilot book that they must anchor 300 yards from the shore of a windswept bay in fifteen metres of turbulent water. The poor buggers must get agoraphobia.

Onwards via the bay of Bømlahamn to Espevær. This collection of small rocky islands about a mile across is another exposed outlier in the Atlantic, but once again with more perfectly sheltered anchorages than the whole of Scotland. We tied up on the quay in the main village next to a 45ft Dutch steel ketch and went for a wander.

The main channel out of Espevaer

In the woods on the other side of the island we came across a lone camping canoeist. This was a man with a canoe, camping in a tent, you understand, not someone paddling a kayak in a particularly effete way. He was striking the camp he'd been in for the past week. A very pleasant little spot to camp. except that he'd been driven half mad by midges and was now heading for home – an island five or six hours to the north. I suggested he hurry since the forecast for the next day was northerly force six, which could be a bit of a strain in a kayak in the open north Atlantic.

Espevær was perhaps the most midgifluous island we visited. Our dinner at a picnic table on the quay had to be cut short as we fled back to the boat and fought over the electric fan – quite an effective means of dispersing the buggers. In a way it was nice to know that there was something to disturb the apparently perfect idyll of the Norwegian islands in the summer. At least the Norges had to suffer midges, like we do.

The skipper of the Dutch boat had been looking at his weather fax and declared that there was unlikely to be enough wind the following day for our sail down to Skudeneshavn – an old haunt from the previous year and starting point for last year's race to Banff.

We sailed on a more-or-less dead run through the rocky islands and round the apparently famously exposed 'Sletta', the last of the 'Dangerous Waves' bits on the charts before I headed across the North Sea again. Goose-winging proved difficult in the rolly conditions and increasing wind. We went down the narrow, canal-like channel through prosperous looking Haugesund town under jib only. It felt more like driving down a wide main shopping street than sailing at sea.

Then we hoisted the main again, expecting light breezes in the sheltered waters

The breeze slowly increased all day until, in the end, we had twenty knots apparent up our jacksie and were surfing along at upwards of seven knots. By the time we arrived at Skudeneshavn the wind was up to a good force six, but you'd hardly have noticed

Espevaer was more like driving through the back streets than sailing

it in the perfectly sheltered guest harbour up its mile long channel through town. Again it felt more like an inland canal than a bit of sea.

The previous year we'd been there during the traditional boat festival and it was almost literally impossible to move. You could have wandered across the harbour at any point over the decks of the thousands of boats in town. This time Skudeneshavn was sleepier and there was plenty of room, albeit that we had to raft up on a Hunter 34 and just next to a small Norwegian yacht rather oddly named 'Dundee'. Though she was probably longer than Zoph she was slightly built and for once another cruising boat was as small, if not smaller than us.

We fired up the laptop and looked for wi-fi in the harbour. We found one hub, entitled 'please ask crew of Dundee for password'. A rather nice, generous gesture on their part.

The following day we motored and motor-sailed in very light conditions to Drivsund. As the breeze went south we sailed, sometimes with the help of a bit of motor. We poked around into three or four anchorages to take a look, but didn't fancy any of them as they were a bit shallow and constrained and exposed to the south. Round the north side of Helgøy were some of the oddest moorings we'd seen. Strings of old truck tyres were simply tied onto low cliff faces on rocky, treed islets. You were clearly just meant to tie directly, beam on, to the rock face, sort of just clamped to the side of an island. We spotted a couple of boats doing this.

Round the north side of the island the buoyage – and indeed the whole topography – had changed out of all recognition from the chart. Helgøy is an island with a population of over fifty, so naturally two causeways were being built, each a mile long, with the sound being bridged in the middle. We carried on between the causeways into the busy pontoons in Helgøysund, which is party island. Apparently major concerts are often held next to the pontoons.

Oddly, electricity on the pontoons was the world's most expensive, at about twelve quid a night, so we didn't indulge. Speaking to an English couple on a wee Hallberg Rassy, they vouchsafed the view that the leccy was so expensive because the place was popular with partygoers. I didn't quite follow the logic, but it must have been unassailable, since the posh bloke, it turned out, was some sort of Naval type working for NATO in Stavanger.

This next bit might worry those of you who are under the delusion that the Navy and the rest of the military consists of a bunch of knowledgeable professionals who are there for your benefit. I found this particular senior naval officer

Langoy

startlingly lacking in fundamental knowledge about modern navigation. During my chat with him he said, as though he'd just had a stroke of rare genius: "Why don't they make – sort of – Tom-Tom devices, like you have in cars, for boats? It'd be good wouldn't it, if you could actually see where you were on a sort of sat-nav sort of device". After some confusion during which I assumed he was making some sort of subtle joke, I pointed out that everyone uses a GPS on boats and that there was, indeed, such a thing as chart plotters. This senior naval officer had genuinely never heard of, or previously considered the possibility of, anyone using a GPS or chartplotter on a boat of any kind.

We had a lazy day the next day as we motored the short distance to the wee island of Langøy, off the larger island of Finnoy, and a facility provided by the Stavanger Sailing Club for the use of its members and visitors. We moored fore and aft to a buoy and the wooden jetty and once again, as we had done last year, marvelled at the open facilities provided. A full sized house lay open, with a large lounge hung with photos of all the past Commodores since Odin. It had a fully equipped kitchen, toilets and showers, bedrooms for those who arrived by dinghy, a gas barbecue area, picnic tables and electricity and water on the quay. All of this was accessible to everyone with payment by honesty box. There was no sign of the razor wire and 'bugger-off' signs which would be de rigueur in privately owned facilities Britain. Once again the rain conspired to arrive after eleven p.m. when we didn't care. I slaughtered Anna at Scrabble yet again.

A rare Stavangan two-Headed Dog

Stav-Anger

Our holiday was coming to an end and we motored in the dreich the next day, checking out a couple of island anchorages on the way to Stavanger to look for somewhere to leave Zoph for a fortnight or so. We went into the biggest local marina, with 500 boats or more, on an island north of Stavanger where a sign in Norwegian suggested that the office was open for one hour only at seven in the evenings.

We went on to Stavanger sailing club, in the busy heart of Stavanger harbour, where a wifey slightly begrudgingly agreed we could leave Zoph for the princely sum of 850 Norks a week. We went back to the first, large marina at seven to catch the office open and did a bit more interpretation of the Norwegian sign. On closer inspection we discovered that the office was open for one hour on Monday evenings only. It proved impossible to do business with this marina, with its bizarrely Scandian opening hours.

So we headed the two miles or so out of town to Lindøy for the night, tying up on the brand new, free wooden jetty next to three or four motorboats. A beautiful little island less than a mile round, Lindøy seems to be council owned and contains an outdoor education centre for kids. Being the middle of the summer of course, this was shut. Tied to the jetty in the middle of nowhere it was difficult to believe that we were only a couple of miles from a major city. The only reminder of civilisation was the considerable disturbance from the wash of hundreds of ferries and other boats passing out in the bay.

I was awoken the next morning by the dawn chorus. I reflected that one really good thing about the North Pole is that you only get one bleeding dawn chorus a year. But the morning was beautiful, hot and sunny so we stayed for a while for sunbathing and swimming.

A huge gaggle of sprogs turned up with their parents in wee speedboats. The fathers scouted along the quay looking up at the low cliffs. Before long they were scaling the cliffs fastening crampons and what have you to them until the cliff was swathed with a variety of climbing ropes. They then forced the male sprogs – between about four and seven years old – to scale the cliffs like wee mountaineers. They are a bit like Kiwis, the Norgians. They can't just go for a walk but need all the right gear to carry out bona-fide

Lindoy: Taking the piss out of funny foreign langauges really is the lowest form of wit

'activities' in the countryside. As soon as they've stopped speeding in boats they shift into another mode that requires a large amount of outdoor equipment. They switch endlessly from fishing to barbecue to climbing to waterskiing and back to fishing again, all done with all the right kit.

Our idyll was slightly marred by the poo-boat. A large landing craft with a crew of four showed up, dislodged a couple of motorboats and muscled into a space on the jetty. The crew proceeded to run a long pipe up to the long-drop public bogs a hundred yards away and pump out all the poo. I was a little perturbed by this – and by the overpowering stench – since I thought these bogs were supposed to compost in-situ.

The crew had dual roles however and one toothless scaffy toured the pleasure boats on the jetty handing out a welcome pack of maps and tourist information detailing all the free moorings with long-drop bogs within fifty miles. Shite pumping and tourist information. A winning combination.

With the evocative stench of sun-drenched defecation lurking in our nostrils we headed back to Stavanger and spent a frustrating hour or so trying to find diesel. This wasn't available in any of the places suggested by either pilot book, both of which are particularly crap on the subject of Stavanger. We finally found some however, then went back to Stavanger Sailing Club and tied Zoph up obsessively with far too many lines in preparation for leaving her for a fortnight.

The more-or-less-permanently-shut approach to business of the big marina, the outdoor centre and various pubs and shops is fairly typical of Norwegian organisations. At the Stavanger Sailing Club we tried to get into their posh club house for a shower – after all we were paying the highest rates in Norway for berthing. A permanent sign proclaimed that the clubhouse was open for one hour on two days each year. That's right, two hours a year. If you were building such a clubhouse you would feel, I imagine, that even if it were to stand for two hundred years it was a bit of a waste of effort and didn't make a lot of economic sense.

Eventually I discovered the clubhouse open and approached the person with the key who had briefly opened it. He agreed that he would let us 'nick a shower' if we were quick. At £15 a day this was a far cry from the practically free fantastic facilities in all the one-horse towns of the north and I was a tad resentful that I was made to feel like I had 'nicked' a shower. Hackles began to rise and I began to experience a little Stav-anger.

We spent a pleasant day and evening in Stavanger however, experiencing, at a price, only the third meal I'd not prepared on Zoph in three months. I found a good chandler and an internet cafe for future reference to check out the weather. I told its Irish proprietor that I'd be back later.

Langoya again

I'd floated low out of Lerwick and not so low to Lofoten. Now Zoph's waterline was frighteningly high. The beer supplies had been running low for a while and over the past week or so I'd been guddling about like a demented squirrel trying to remember where he'd buried all his acorns last autumn. Now I had exhausted even the supplies of Boddingtons buried in the smelly hole under the bog. I had to face the fact that I was, tragically, down to one remaining can of beer of the 450 cans and 200 bottles I'd started with. The forty litres of spirits were seriously depleted as well. I took some small solace from the remaining five litres of vodka which were virtually the only supplies of alcohol left.

The following day we flew back from Stavanger to Newcastle on our cheapo internet tickets. It was August 10th and I'd been on board since May 28th, travelling on Zoph a total of 2055 miles since I'd last joined her in Lerwick and 2380 miles from Port Edgar. Of course it took about an hour to fly back. I wonder if Columbus, had he the opportunity to fly about in jumbo jets at hundreds of miles an hour, would understand our insistence at exploring the planet at roughly the speed he did. I suspect, given the choice, he'd have become a frequent flyer.

It is a constant source of wonder to me that there are people in this world who will voluntarily fly to Norway just to sail across the North Sea in a twenty seven foot boat at walking pace. Thank goodness there are such people however and my crew for the crossing this time was Mary Watson and Norman Weibye. Both were members of Port Edgar Yacht Club and Norman is of Norgian stock and speaks the language. This ought to be a useful trait but in a country in which practically everyone speaks perfect English is in fact scarcely necessary.

I flew back to Stavanger the day before they were due to arrive and moved Zoph into the city guest harbour with its pay and display parking, to await their arrival. Anxious for accurate weather forecasts I went back to the internet cafe I'd checked out two weeks before. It was not only shut but shut down. Peering through the window I could see that it was empty of computers and furniture. I did tell the bloke I'd be back later, but I suppose I didn't say it'd be two weeks later.

A British cruise liner managed, unsurprisingly, to annoy the hell out of me in Stavanger. The modern tower block cruise liner is an aesthetic nightmare. Yu really ought to need planning permission to build fifteen storey tower blocks, even if they are floating. Often they display a peculiar arrogance by sounding their foghorns on departing from harbours, even if it's four in the morning. "Look at me, look at me!"

P&O liners are particularly arrogant. One arrived in Stavanger's deep but narrow inner city harbour. This is about ninety metres across. Moored ships of at least twenty metres beam line both sides. This leaves a channel a maximum of fifty metres wide into the harbour. All day hundreds of commercial and leisure boats swarm through this only corridor into the city's main harbour.

As is their wont, once tied up alongside this P&O liner hung a huge banner along her side which read "Do not approach within 50 metres!" Happily nobody seemed to take any notice of this notice and the normal shipping movements continued. Imagine having such an inflated sense of your own importance that you would arrive in a foreign country and immediately seek to lay down the law about where the locals are allowed to go. If I'd been a local I'd have scuttled the bloody thing. My hackles rose with renewed Stav-anger.

I found internet access in the public library and did some planning. Zoph is a seaworthy sort of boat but she is only twenty seven feet, so I'm a bit obsessive about picking and choosing the right conditions for major sea crossings. Horror stories from the previous year's North Sea race from Stavanger to Banff made me unapologetic about my wimpy approach. Though the current conditions appeared fine, we were expecting some strong westerlies. I reckoned that if we waited a couple of days we'd get a short period of very light wind, followed by decent sized breezes from the south. The others, when they arrived at lunchtime the next day concurred and we sailed slowly north in the sun for Langøya again, buoyed by my stories of the fantastic facilities available.

Arriving at Langøya we had the place to ourselves. What I hadn't considered was the possibility that, when nobody was there from the Stavanger Sailing Club, all the facilities would be securely locked up and the leccy switched off. What a bummer.

Tananger

Morale improved a little however as we managed to improvise. I found an obscure socket high up outside the club house under the eaves and we just managed an improbably long connection using all the wire we had on board, stretched tight and crossing hills and valleys between Zoph and the back of the clubhouse. Showering was achieved by dint of swimming in the sea then dousing under a cold hosepipe on the quay. Though a method more appropriate to the tropics than the latitude of Shetland it was, I can report, surprisingly acceptable. Mary could also report this, since she went for the cold shower but Norman, who wimped out and remained wholly unwashed, couldn't.

The next day, with predicted strong westerlies, we wanted to make for the coastal town of Tananger in preparation for starting our crossing the following day. We had a gentle beat but the wind shifted slowly from southerly round to westerly and we ended up motoring to windward in heavy rain. If truth be told it was one of the more miserable passages of the summer. As we cleared the point north west of Stavanger however and turned south towards Tananger in waters more exposed to the north sea, the waves and the wind got up and we had a fast, exhilarating sail with two reefs in the main. It was good for the others to experience a bit of proper sailing in proper sea and get used to Zoph before we started out on the real thing.

We arrived in Tananger soaked to the skin in a wholly unreasonably heavy rain shower. Though fifteen or sixteen miles from Stavanger by sea, Tananger is about four miles and fifteen minutes away by land and feels like it, since it is rather suburban and lacking any apparent life of its own. It's a pleasant enough place however, as is virtually everywhere in Norway. There are shops and the hotel provided Norman with free wi-fi access for more obsessive checking of the weather. The harbour has more of the feel of a passage harbour than other places I'd been of late, with a couple of German yachts, a Dutchster and a posh southern English yacht in town, waiting for suitable weather windows.

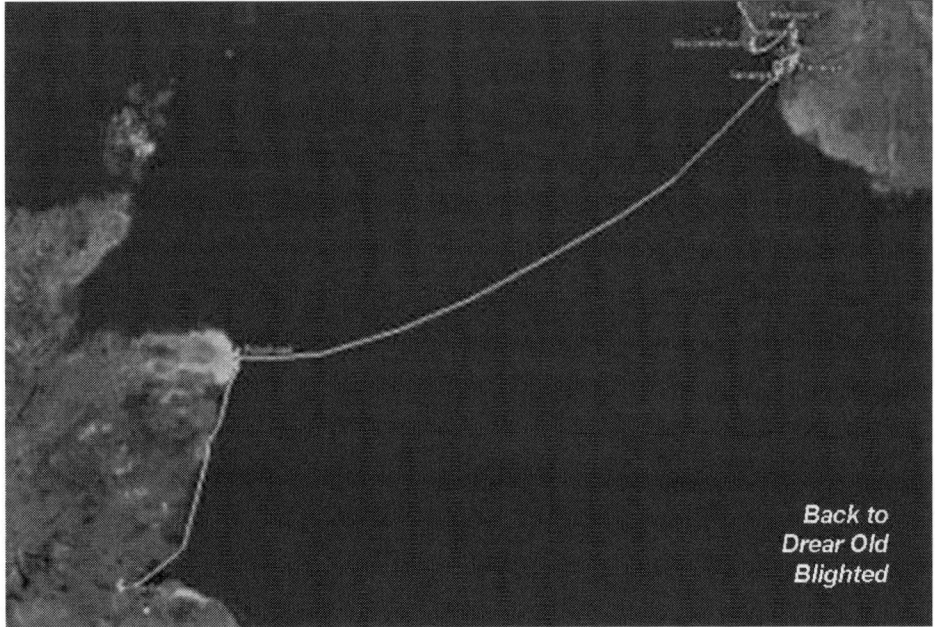

*Back to
Drear Old
Blighted*

Drear Old Blighted

At 8.45 the following morning we bit the bullet and headed west out of Tananger, into what was left of the westerlies and the steep chop they had created, at the start of our North Sea crossing. We began with two reefs in the main and motored off, slamming into the waves and wind. It was a bit of an inauspicious start.

Soon however the wind backed a bit, we shook out the reefs and had a sail for an hour or two, until Norway faded and disappeared into the distance behind us. After a while the breeze wasn't enough to overcome the swell and with the boom tending to thrash about a bit we ended up motorsailing once again.

The conditions were pretty benign but nevertheless a bit annoying. There was a two metre swell from the west, but wee waves interfering with this from all over the place, primarily the south. This had Zoph rolling about slightly unpleasantly and made it difficult to sleep, set appropriate sail or make tea. At night the breeze went easterly and we had a go at sailing, but again it was too rolly and we ended up centring the boom and tying it back to the boom gallows to stop it thrashing about.

Apart from the odd ship on the AIS there was basically bugger-all to see for the first hundred miles or so, but on the second morning we passed a platform in the Leipner oil field and after that there was pretty much always an oil rig to be seen somewhere. I'd not crossed the North Sea so far south before and was surprised at how much stuff there was out there. We'd been heading directly to Peterhead so far, avoiding the stronger winds further south. After Leipner we decided to head southwards, steering about 240° towards Port Edgar. This was because the breeze was due to strengthen from the south – perhaps reaching up to a force six – in a couple of days. As we approached closer to Scotland this would enable us to bear away from the increasing wind and head more or less

due west to Peterhead, which bears about 255° from Tananger.

From about three pm on the second day things improved considerably. The sky cleared to sunbathing weather and the swell from the west subsided. The dolphin display teams – seemingly always sticking to the UK sector – came to give us a show in the early evening.

But after about ten that evening was the best bit. The breeze came in steadily from the south, allowing us to sail at five to six knots under full sail in a force four. The phosphorescent plankton lit up the sea. This was the first time I'd seen this ubiquitous phenomenon this year. Earlier on the sun had been shining all night and latterly there was always electric light around, which overwhelmed the shining plankton.

As well as sea-plankt the sky-plankt was out in profusion. A trillion stars lit up the moonless sky. I'm so used to seeing a few insipid stars against a yellowish urban background that I expect to be able to identify stuff like the Plough. That night the sky was so incandescent with stars that it was hard to identify the familiar ones. Living in our modern, electrically lit world it's easy to forget just how many of the buggers there are up there.

For a few minutes around midnight we had dolphins jumping through the sea-plankt around Zoph's speeding bow wave. Their shapes were brightly lit up by the disturbed plankt whilst their glistening bodies were lit from above by the sky-plankt. It was an experience that's difficult to beat.

After midnight the breeze increase to a bit over twenty knots. By day I wouldn't have bothered but because it was a dark night and we were on solo watches I tucked a couple of reefs in the main. We continued through the night at six knots. Our more southerly course was paying off as we described a gentle curve up towards Peterhead. Various points on the horizon were lit by the loom of oil rigs pissing our fossil fuel up into the night sky in flares and arc lights. We knew they were thirty or forty miles away, but each one obscured all the stars from its own bit of horizon.

Around three a.m. on my watch, we passed through what I took to be a fishing fleet, though no fishing lights were showing on the slowly, somewhat erratically moving ships. As we were on a collision course with one of them and had right of way I shone a large torch at them for a few seconds. Perhaps they'd not seen our puny tricolour light as they peered out from their Christmas-tree-lit ship. Amazingly this tactic seemed to work and they immediately changed course. Most ships are so lit up at night that you can hardly make out their nav lights and they are unlikely to pick out a wee thing like the tricolour on a sailing boat.

Soon after this I retired to my pit, leaving Mary and subsequently Norman to steer us within sight of Peterhead. The motion was much more pleasant than the previous night and I slept pretty well for four hours or so. Rising I took a quick squint at the chart plotter and decided quickly that there was something

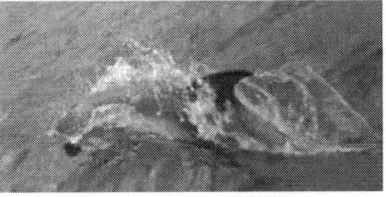

seriously wrong with the GPS. Over the last couple of hours we had apparently followed a course some thirty degrees further to the north than we should have been. A little investigation demonstrated that it was us and not the GPS that had gone wrong. Propelled by a strong ebb tide as we neared the coast we were heading to round Rattray head at over six knots and had been for two hours.

I brought us back on course, involving a stiff beat against the tide at two and a half knots. We decided to cut our losses and motor-sail to Peterhead. Our nice southerly cushion, cunningly gained over two days, had been lost in a couple of hours and the last ten miles was spent battering slowly against wind and tide to Peterhead. Some frenetic lessons were imparted to a member of the crew on the difference between compass course, heading and course over the ground, the virtues of looking at the course on the GPS occasionally and the effects of both leeway and tide. The point was forcibly made that maximising speed over the ground may be an inappropriate course of action if you are heading down tide and in entirely the wrong direction.

We made our UK landfall in Peterhead at nine thirty am on August 30th, 112 days since my last visit. Zoph was back in Drear Old Blighted at last.

Unfortunately we were so pleased with ourselves after the crossing that we told the bloke in the marina we'd arrived from Norway and he made us fill in a customs form. Entering the country through Peterhead Marina is however considerably more pleasant than doing so at an airport, since it doesn't involve the now customary strip-search and anal probing. Indeed the bloke seemed refreshingly unconcerned whether we filled in the forms right or whether – horror of horrors – we were travelling under false names.

We filled up with diesel. After having the motor on for three quarters of the journey and spending two days motoring in Norway before we left, we had used fifty eight litres of diesel - about 40% of a tank – to go 283 miles. Not much more than a litre an hour.

I'd phoned the Shoreside Logistics Team (Anna) a couple of hours before arriving in Peterhead and prevailed upon her to give us a lift back to Edinburgh. The forecast strong southerlies for the next couple of days had persuaded me to leave Zoph in Peterhead for a while. We didn't have to wait long until she appeared. Anna drove back to Edinburgh as we three sat by turns gormless and fast asleep after our crossing. A couple of days as part of a crew of three knackers me. God knows how the solo round the world obsessives manage it.

With a forecast of light westerlies for a couple of days followed by stronger easterlies, I travelled back to Peterhead and on the morning of September 3rd motored out of the harbour a mile or so behind a nice big steel Dutch yacht from Leiden. Even a couple of years earlier a trip of 115 miles from Peterhead to Port Ed would have taken on epic proportions in my mind. After this year's voyage it felt like just a wee local trip. Zoph was almost home.

The breeze wasn't supposed to be in the South East, but it was and that was no bad thing as I had a good fine reach for a bit, with up to two knots of tide helping. The wind was even more in defiance of the forecast for the last couple of hours to Stonehaven as it veered south and increased to fifteen to twenty three knots apparent. A wet blatter motorsailing to Stonehaven against a significant chop ensued. In the harbour thirty or forty dinghy sailors were complaining that there'd probably not be enough wind to sail. It was a rare but good sight to see so many boats out sailing from Stonehaven, which is normally full of boats which appear never to leave the harbour.

In the morning I was nobbled by the harbour master for sixteen quid. After Norway it seemed a heavy price to pay for rubbing up against a wall covered in shackles and lumps of metal in a harbour with all the facilities locked up which becomes untenable in strong easterlies. Welcome back to Britain.

The same weather pattern was repeated the following day as I motorsailed the fifty miles to Anstruther. Unfortunately I had tide against me for the first few hours, but speed improved as the tide turned. Again the wind increased to fifteen knots apparent from the south, but there was no significant chop, even as I passed through a fleet of a dozen or so fishing boats round Fife Ness. Turning west I got out full sail and had a great wee reach at up to seven knots to Anstruther.

In Anstruther I tied up to one of their drying pontoons at first, but with the harbour master away at five pm there was no way to and from the pontoons through the security gates. A party of considerably pissed old blokes celebrating a seventy fifth birthday on one of the boats tried to be helpful but couldn't get their heads round the concept of needing to get in and out of the marina, since they had always had keys. I moved over to the harbour wall and tied up, waiting to go aground at low tide.

Mary Watson and her other half Charlie Hussey joined me for the last night and the run to Port Ed. After a pub dinner Charlie and I had to slacken off the shrouds as Zoph leaned rather too heavily onto the wall and the shrouds came under pressure on it.

We remembered to re-tighten them the next morning before motoring out of the harbour at eight am. I didn't remember to check the split pins however, which nearly ended in disaster the following Sunday, when the starboard shroud just fell off whilst sailing in a near gale out of Port Ed. But that's another story.

The forecast was for light westerlies increasing all day and, for once, this proved entirely accurate. We started out sailing at about two and a half knots against the tide in very light breezes. Racing skipper Charlie did not, as I'd anticipated he might, try to persuade me to hoist the cruising 'chute, for which I was later grateful.

The breeze increased infinitesimally slowly and steadily all day. There were no gusts, just a very steadily increasing easterly which started out at force one. It was up to a force four by the time, twenty miles out, that we could first glimpse the Forth rail and road bridges. By the time we rounded the island of Inchkeith, eight miles from the bridges, it was up to a force five. I reflected that, viewed from Port Edgar in a force five or six, Inchkeith normally seems a million miles away and a trip round it quite an adventure. Returning from the high Arctic Inchkeith looked like my welcoming front doorstep.

We ran fast up past Inchkeith and underneath the bridges, tying up on pontoon D22 at three p.m. on September the fifth, with the wind still increasing. Within half an hour of arriving I was watching the peculiar Port Edgar ballet of boats pitching and rolling in an easterly near gale, their masts clanging noisily together and bits of anemometer and tricolour light flying around the harbour.

Anstruther approach

Postscript

And that was it. Home at last. Zoph had been away exactly four months to the day since the Tuesday morning I'd left saying that I'd most probably be back the same evening. During that time we'd sailed, motorsailed or motored a total of exactly 2800 miles in 83 days sailing.

Importantly and incredibly - we still had a couple of bottles of gin and half a bottle of whisky left, but disturbingly, no beer.

I had time to ponder on lessons learned from the trip. Firstly, take plenty of beer with you. Secondly, don't ram dirty great rocks. Thirdly, if you insist on hitting a rock then do so in Norway. Fourthly, if you don't take plenty of beer then don't not take it to Norway.

Would I recommend acquiring a small yacht and taking it to Norway? Well the next time you suggest to your other half that you need a new boat and they start arguing that you can't afford it, consider this.

I reckoned that in 2008 a holiday for a couple travelling round Norway without your own yacht would cost about £140 a day for accommodation, £20 a day for car hire, about the same for petrol, a conservative £60 a day for evening meals and £40 a day for lunch. Allowing for just four small drinks each a day it would be about £64 a day for booze. Then there's say £400 for flights and at least £1000 for the inevitable ferry trips to get around the islands. The total cost without your own yacht of a ninety day stay in Norway would be at least £32,360, not including any incidental expenses and luxuries.

On the other hand, my 90 day stay in Norway cost me about £2,000 all in. Zoph cost £20,000 to buy. So over the summer of 2008 alone the boat paid for herself <u>and</u> made a clear profit of £10,360.

So if your other half argues that you can't afford a boat, tell them that in these days of credit-crunching and tightening of belts, it would be irresponsible economic suicide <u>not</u> to buy a yacht.

So, the end of the trip, the end of holidays, the end of summer. A long, dark winter of firesides and sitting indoors stretched ahead. Oh, except of course for my trip on Equinox from Portugal to the Caribbean in November and December. I hurried home to buy tickets for the Algarve. Well, it's not exactly as though I get a lot of chances to go sailing, is it?

Oh, by the way, I said at the start of all this that only one person in Norway recognised Zoph as a Vancouver. It was in Bødo. I was just bringing Zoph back onto the pontoon after a Swedish boat had left. An old chap got off 'Bamsen', the 62ft Hallberg Rassy next door and came to help with my lines. He tied up the bow and I tied up the stern. As I went to take the line from him and thank him he said "Is that a Vancouver?" "Yes" I said "...are you Mr Rassy?" "Ja" he said. And he was.

Christoph Rassy, the founder and owner of Scandinavia's biggest and best known builder of really high quality, expensive yachts, was the only person to recognise wee Zoph. I told you it was someone of discernment.

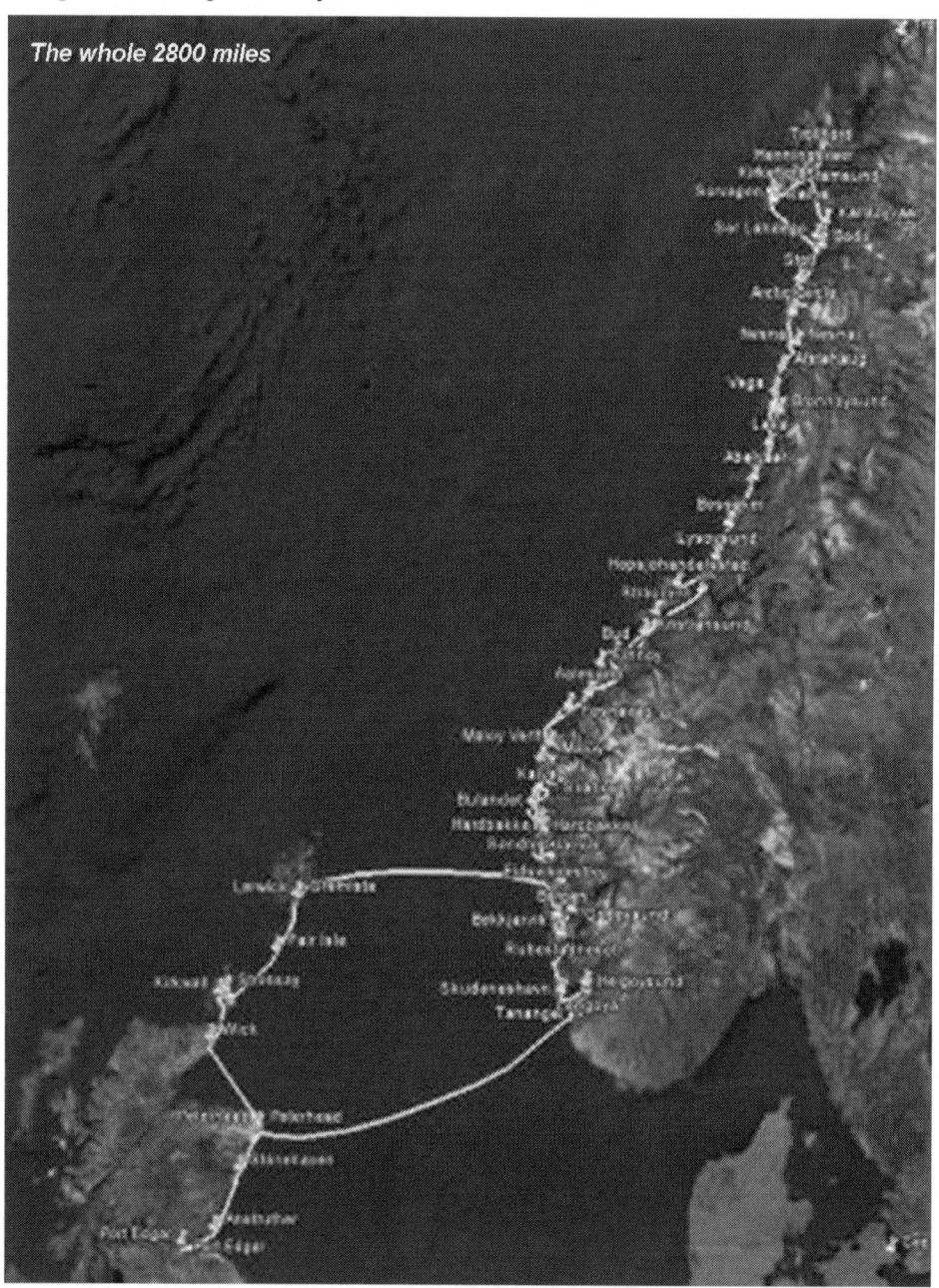

The whole 2800 miles

This is one of four books so far describing Zophiel's cruises.

"Skagerrak and Back: Zophiel's Two Summer Cruises in 2007" is the first one and is a relatively short account of a North Sea circuit.

"Floating Low to Lofoten" describes her trip from Edinburgh north to the Norwegian arctic and back in 2008.

"A Gigantic Whinge on the Celtic Fringe: A Total and Complete Circumnavigation of Ireland and Britain by the Slightly Truncated Irish Route" is, if you can get past the misleading title, just about a trip around Ireland in 2011.

"Bobbing to the Baltic" is the tale of her 2012 trip along much the same route as described in Griff Rhys Jones' book 'To the Baltic with Bob', but with a pile more photos and descriptions of a lot more good places to stop.

I have also written two books about my travels – without Zophiel – in parts of Asia, Africa and Central America little frequented by Europeans. They are entitled *"Travels with my Rant"* and *"The Front of Beyond"*.

There's more sailing tales at **http://www.edge.me.uk/Sailinghome.htm**, where you will also find the colour photos contained in these volumes.

Printed in Great Britain
by Amazon

35633427R00073